THUMBS OUT

THUMBS OUT

Jim Poole

*Memories of growing up on a mink farm
in a small New England town during
the Depression, World War II,
grades 1-12 in Sudbury schools,
UVM, U.S. Army service,
marriage and coming home.*

This book is based on the author's memories of growing up many years ago and, therefore, is as accurate as possible.

Second Edition Paperback
ISBN 978-1-329-87431-2

First Edition Hardback
ISBN 978-1-329-82682-3

In memory of Wendy

Dedicated to Our Grandchildren

Kelsey Ann Flagg
Morgan Sarah Flagg
Veronica McCarthy Mann
Savanna Merril Poole
Marina Grace Poole
Tyler James Mann
Schuyler Elizabeth Farrell
Natalie Wendel Farrell
Will Thomas Farrell

Our Children

Dirk Daniel Poole
Kristen Flagg
Ann Wahlers Mann
Sally Weatherwax Farrell

This is how things were when I was growing up.
As always, many things have changed...
some worse and some better.

Many of my varied interests and accomplishments to date are listed on the opposite page... I have worn and continue to wear many hats.

Mink Farmer

Carpenter

Electrician

Bulldozer Operator

Excavator Operator

Tractor Operator

Wheelbarrow Operator

Latin Scholar

Truck Driver

Tractor-Trailer Driver

Airplane Mechanic

Inventor: Truck trailer steering apparatus, U.S. Patent No. 6,152,475, Nov. 28, 2000

Author

Ready to go...

CONTENTS

My mother and me

Framingham Union Hospital was relatively close
to where my family lived in Sudbury.
There was no hospital in Sudbury, so Framingham
or Sudbury could be claimed as place of birth.

BEFORE SCHOOL
summer 1932–summer 1938

MY BABY BOOK

I am sitting at home by the woodstove on a stormy November day in 2014 on River Road in Newcastle, Maine. On my lap is a pink baby book, my baby book, with photos. Didn't they know that blue is for boys and pink is for girls?

Place of Birth: *Framingham, Massachusetts*

Date: *Wednesday, July 6, 1932 at 11 a.m.*

Parents: *Claude Randall Poole*
and Dorothy Weatherwax Poole

Me: *James Edward Poole*

I've arrived. Here we go!

1

Grampa Edd Poole proudly holding me and standing next to Gramma Bertha Poole with Nancy tilting her baby carriage and paying no attention to me or her grandparents or the photographer (probably Dad). On this trip to visit us they traveled from Iowa on U.S. Route 20 in their Ford, seen in the background.

PARENTS & GRANDPARENTS

My parents came from Iowa: Diagonal and Waterloo.

My father, Claude Randall Poole, was nicknamed Jim and his father's name was Edd, so that is how they came up with naming me James Edward.

My paternal grandparents, Edd and Bertha Poole, lived in Diagonal, a small town in southern Iowa named for a place where two railroads crossed at a diagonal. Edd said Iowa is where the tall corn grows. He bought railroad cars of sheep or hogs and finished them—that is, fed them—until they were ready to send to market in Chicago.

 My mother, Dorothy Louise Weatherwax, was born and lived in Waterloo. Her father, Herbert Weatherwax, owned an insurance agency where she worked while she was growing up. Herbert died before I was born. I am sitting on Grandma Jennie Weatherwax's lap at left. She died before I was old enough to remember her.

In 1925 Mom graduated from Grinnell College in Grinnell, Iowa, and Dad graduated from the University of Iowa in Iowa City.

Dad went on to work in the oil fields for Phillips Petroleum Company and knew Mr. Phillips. When Mom and Dad were first married, after a stint in Bartlesville, Oklahoma, they moved to Bound Brook, New Jersey. It was there that Dad managed a Philfuels distribution plant. His next position was the same type of job with Philgas in Sudbury, Massachusetts. They arrived in Sudbury in 1930, the day after the old Town Hall burned to the ground and just before my sister Nancy was born on April 4.

3

SUDBURY, WHERE I GREW UP

Sudbury, Massachusetts, where I was born, was a small town 20 miles west of Boston. When I was young, Sudbury was the carnation growing center of the world. There were at least 10 large greenhouses growing carnations for the Boston flower market, a few small dairy farms, three large chicken farms, three pig farms and three mink farms.

I wanted to celebrate and arrive on July 4, 1932, but Mom wouldn't co-operate. She kept me cozy warm and in the dark for two more days until July 6. My parents decided to keep me along with my two-year-old sister, Nancy Jane.

We lived downstairs in a rented two-family home on Landham Road. Catherine and Dan Blue lived upstairs. As I grew older I would hear Mrs. Blue mixing cake batter.

I would run upstairs saying, "Miss-a-boo, Miss-a-boo, can I have a wick?"

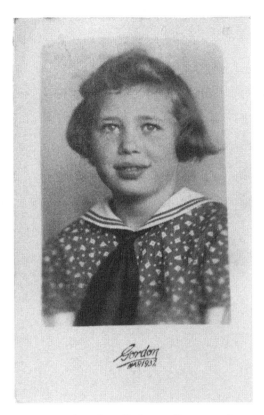

Nancy's school photo, first grade

SISTER NANCY

Nancy, being two years older, headed off to first grade at school where she became a star pupil while I stayed home.

My days without her were busy. I was an outdoor explorer as often as possible, interested in seeing what excitement I could get into that often involved various pets and mink, whatever was fair game for an imaginative four- and five-year-old to take on.

Wearing my gas station grease hat and riding Queeny

FIRST PETS

Dad liked to hunt and fish. My first pets were Joe and Babe, old-fashioned black-and-tan foxhounds. Next came another black-and-tan, Old Nick, from Clinton, Mass., which was about 30 miles away. As soon as Nick arrived, he ran back home. He did this twice. We finally explained to him that he was our dog, he belonged to us and should stay with us in his new home in Sudbury. Nick finally agreed.

Queeny the horse was in the twilight years of her life. When she would lie down, it would take three or four men to help her stand up. If she got loose, she would go next door to the Johnson farm to visit their horses. At six years old, I would go there and lead her home. I could barely reach her halter, but traffic on Landham Road was not a problem— there was hardly any.

A RESEARCHER'S MIND
91 GALLONS

My parents told me that my birthday, July 6, 1932, was the stock market's lowest day during the Great Depression in the United States. To tell the truth, that didn't bother me. I was setting out to be a scientist or someone who solves problems.

One question intrigued me: "How much does a person pee in a year?"*

My friend Bobby lived across the street. He was willing to help with the experiment, but my arithmetic skills were nonexistent. If there were two of us, we would have to add the total amount and divide the results by two. Anyway, back to the story.

Our experiment began. We had a playroom down in the cellar with just an old rug on the floor and some shelves that held canned goods and empty Ball glass canning jars. Time went by, but not even close to a year.

One day Mom came down, opened a jar and screamed, **"WHAT IS THAT SMELL?!"**

Busted!

"Take all those glass jars out to the dump, and be sure to BREAK all of them!" Mom instructed.

In those days, most homes had their own dump. Breaking glass jars was something we could do. Little did Mom know that she was encouraging me to have a satisfying youthful career in breaking glass.

Another researcher, Linda Mueller, solved the problem as I was remembering and writing this: "91 Gallons!" (Thank you, Linda.)

Nancy, Dad and me

EARLY MINK HOBBY &
QUITTING A JOB

Dad started raising mink as a hobby in 1936. At that time there was no such thing as a mink industry. There were fox farms scattered around the United States and Canada, but not mink. Initially Dad had 10 mink in 10 huge individual pens. He then built a wooden mink house. This first shed had about 15 wire pens outside on each side, each with a water cup attached at the end. Each pen included a nest box inside. We had access to mink in these pens from an inside walkway down the middle of the wooden house *(see photo next page.)*

In the beginning, we had two pigs that ate leftover mink food—always mostly fish. But when the pigs were butchered the pork tasted so fishy we couldn't eat it.

At some point in the late 1930's, Dad was offered a promotion to manage a Philgas plant in Detroit. This was during the Depression when jobs were scarce. Dad didn't want Philgas to tell him what to do or where to move or work ever again. He quit his job and started selling real estate and insurance, with Mom doing most of the insurance work.

I am just guessing, but I'm pretty sure that in 1938 Dad decided to go into mink farming full time. So while he was busy with the real estate and insurance business, he was enlarging the herd and learning the ins and outs of mink farming. He needed help, and Nancy and I were ready.

Here I am on the doorstep of one of the early wooden mink houses, posing for the photo.

FARMHANDS

I became more useful when I was five and could help with the pelting. Outside in the mink yard a crate of mink was put into a killing box that was connected to the exhaust pipe of an idling car. After a couple minutes I was told to turn off the ignition key. The mink were dumped out on a skinning table. My job was to hold one of the back paws while Dad held the other and made a cut between them. Next step, I held both back paws while Dad held the base of the tail and made a triangle cut, so the mink was ready to be skinned. In all the

10

years since, that procedure remained the same.

By the summer I turned six, I had more serious responsibilities. Each pen held one mink and each pen had a water cup that MUST have water. Watering was always the first and last thing to do every day. On hot summer days we watered often during midday. Nancy did lots of watering, but if Dad was away or busy I helped her. Our watering cans were retired later when an automatic watering system was in place.

I always was told, "**DON'T** put your fingers in the mink pen—they bite!" My whole life, whenever I heard **DON'T**, I had to find out **WHY**. I would have been O.K. except for the **DON'Ts**.

One warm summer day a mink was sound asleep, and I thought I was faster than the mink. I poked my finger up through the pen bottom for just an instant. Nothing! She was still sound asleep (or so I thought) so I tried again. Still no movement, still sleeping. On my third try, she was ready, and I quickly removed my bleeding finger from the pen. I remember hiding my hand under the table at supper time. It was bad enough to get bitten, but I avoided grief from my parents and "I told you **DON'T**" at all costs.

Another time I was barefoot (I was always barefoot) in the mink house, and a mother mink was loose. She was probably protecting her litter, otherwise she would have run away. This time, she bit my foot and held onto the tendons on top of my foot, the ones going to the toes. My father picked me up, and I saw the mink holding onto my foot. Finally, Dad kicked it off. Because she was holding onto tendons, she didn't rip the skin open. I was fine until "they" (you know who) decided that the cut needed iodine. Iodine was always worse than any injury itself. I'm still proud of four little scars on my foot.

11

RELATIVES & THE ROUND ROBIN

Mom's family news traveled in the "Round Robin" via the U.S. Post Office. A bulging envelope circled from Mom in Sudbury to her brother in Illinois, on to her sister in Iowa, then to her brother in California and finally back to her. Each family added a newsy letter and removed the one that had made the rounds.

Uncle Robert and Aunt Corinne both worked in Chicago. He was in charge of the elevators in one of Chicago's tall office buildings, a skyscraper. Back then operators ran elevators, announced the floors, and caused the doors to open and close—no push-it-yourself floor buttons. Many elevators had a small fold-down stool for the elevator operator to sit on during slower times of the day.

U.S. Route 20 spanned the country—Massachusetts to Oregon—through Sudbury and by Aunt Maud Shane's house on Independence Avenue in Waterloo. Her house had no front driveway access. A back alley served garages, garbage pickup, the milk man and so forth for her and other families on her block and the block behind her. The Shanes had a two-car garage on the alley with a model A Ford in it. Uncle Charles was a dentist. Cousin Dick worked at Black's Department Store. Cousin Herb was studying to be an architect. He had polio as a child and limped slightly.

Rath Meatpacking Company of Waterloo packed pork meat products; Mom knew the Rath family. The John Deere factory was there. You could order a John Deere tractor, travel to the factory to watch it being made and then drive it off the assembly line. That would have been a treat!

Uncle Edwin, Aunt Roberta, and Cousin Bob lived in North Hollywood, California. They added a letter—family news had made the rounds—and sent the R.R. back East.

AUNT MAUD & UNCLE CHARLES
VISIT AND GO TO BOSTON

Aunt Maud and Uncles Charles Shane sometimes drove East to visit us and see the sights. Mom was always happy to act as tour director. In Boston Uncle Charles let the women off to see some historical highlight and said he would drive around the block and then pick them up.

That works in Midwest cities, but not in downtown Boston where one-way streets were laid out on crooked Colonial cow paths. Mom and Aunt Maud were never found again.

Just kidding, but it did take a long time to "get around the block." *It reminds me of poor Charlie on the MTA.*

RUNNING BOARDS

Which also reminds me that early in the 1930's cars had running boards. When you drove through Boston slowly as though you were looking for something, such as Paul Revere's house, a young boy would jump on the running board, hold on and ask where you wanted to go. You then had your own personal guide to places in the city. When you got where you wanted to be, you gave him a small tip.

Bring back running boards!

BEST TOY

Another memory of the problem-solver's cellar playroom was my best toy ever! It was a Buddy-L truck with real working headlights. I had so much fun with the headlights on and the cellar light off! I'm sure the batteries didn't last as long as they do nowadays.

A NAP TO REMEMBER

One of my first memories: I thought that if something involved my life, I should know best. I was encouraged to take an afternoon nap. "Encouraged" is not the right word. The truth was that Mom wanted and needed me to nap.

I disagreed strongly. In protest, I scratched a picture of a snowman into the maple headboard and then took off all the bedding including the mattress and scattered everything all over the bedroom.

I don't remember the aftermath of this little episode, but she didn't give me away so I must have been O.K. to keep.

*Playing on the front porch with Nancy before I was old
enough (trustworthy enough?) to play in the cellar*

15

My school photo, first grade

OUR FIRST GRADE OPENING SONG

Good morning to you.
Good morning to you.
We're all in our places
With sunshiny faces.
Oh, this is the way
To start a new day.

FIRST & SECOND GRADES
fall 1938–spring 1940

SOUTH SCHOOL

I don't remember wanting or not wanting to go to school. My sister Nancy loved school and excelled. She went half a year in first grade, moved to the other side of the room for half a year in second grade, and at the end of her first school year was promoted to third grade. So although only two years older, Nancy was three grades ahead of me in fourth grade when I started first grade.

Mrs. Johnson, my first—and second—grade teacher, was a widow in the later years of her life. She was kind, stern, and able to successfully teach two grades in a single classroom. We learned a lot.

South School had two large rooms with a hall between them and outside doors at each end of the hall. When you entered, grades one and two were in the room to the left and grades three and four to the right. Each classroom had two coat rooms, one for the girls and one for the boys. The toilets were downstairs in the basement—again, one for the girls and one for the boys. Toilets were used after a 15-minute morning recess and after a 30-minute noontime lunch period.

17

GETTING READY

Preparing for first grade at South School meant shopping for a new outfit. I wasn't used to having an entire new outfit all at once. I got a new pair of knickers with knee length stockings and a polo shirt.

New shoes were a chore after being barefoot all summer. At the shoe store there was an x-ray machine. You put your feet inside, looked down into a viewer on the machine, saw your bones within the shoes and decided if the shoes fit correctly and if there was enough room for growth. These machines were later removed from stores; the x-rays were dangerous.

FIRST GRADE

I remember Marcia Gaughan from early in first grade and probably knew her before school started.

Anyway, Marcia and I had most of the same classes from first grade through high school. We had dancing classes with Hollywood Haynes, took college-prep courses, and acted in the senior plays.

I was jealous of Marcia. When we were assigned seatwork—cutting and pasting—hers would come out neat and tidy, but not mine.

BATHROOM PROCEDURES: "THUMBS OUT!"

The boys' bathroom routine was serious business that required Mrs. Johnson as both warden and overseer of three student monitors (being a monitor was a rotating job). The separate toilet area consisted of two urinals (firsts) and two stalls (third and fourth).

For each boy waiting patiently in line with his hands in his pockets, Mrs. J. required **"THUMBS OUT!"**

The first monitor stood by to keep the flow of boys steady. After each use, the monitor inspected for "spots." If you failed and left spots, you went out to the wastebasket at the sink, got a used paper towel and went back to wipe up the spots before the line could move.

Boys in the second line stopped to wash their hands at the sink. Here was monitor number two. He was the "towel puller," one towel per boy. After you tossed the used paper towel in the wastebasket, you joined line number three.

This was the line for the water fountain. God forbid that you should get a normal drink of water. The third monitor determined how much water you got.

Being monitor was a real position of power. The first monitor could send kids back to wipe up spots or let them go according to whether he was friend or foe. Controlling the water fountain was the same—a satisfying drink or not.

I still follow the rule: **THUMBS OUT!**

MY JOB

I had a seat in the back row, next to the door. If anyone knocked, my job was to open the door. I have no memory of ever opening the door for anyone... except Mrs. Bartlett, a School Board member, who came once.

HURRICANE OF 1938

It started out as a nice bright September day, *no hurricane warnings then like we would receive today.* I was six and had just started school. Nancy and I were at home playing outside in the garage. It was windy enough that we thought it would be fun to build a kite to fly. *Back then one didn't go to the store and buy one.* As we got out our kite-building supplies, nails were blowing all around the floor!

We never finished the kite.

By supper time, the wind was approaching full force. My friend Bobby, from across the street, was outside and was leaning way over and could barely stand up. Why couldn't I go out? No fun staying in with Mom and Nancy. We were in the bedroom, and just then the window blew in—glass all over the place. I had a cut on my hip, just big enough to brag about. Dad and Dan Blue quickly got an old door—*no plywood then*—and tacked it up over the broken window.

Next, a large maple tree blew down across Landham Road. Dad and Dan came to the rescue again. They decided they could saw it off at the stump, but they didn't know how to move it off the road. They found a two-man saw, *in the days before chainsaws*, and started. As soon as the tree was sawn through, the wind blew it off the road!

A little later, we received word that the Bordens' cow barn had blown down and they needed help to get the cows out. Dad went out to the call, but they didn't need help from any six-year-old.

This hurricane of September 18, 1938, left hundreds dead along the East Coast. The damage was tremendous all the way up the coast from New York City through Connecticut, Rhode Island, Massachusetts and Maine. Electricity was out for three weeks.

We rode around afterward, amazed to see the damage to trees, homes and barns. Unfortunately, South School, my school in South Sudbury, had no damage. Some damage and days off would have been exciting.

Henry Ford, founder of Ford Motor Company, used lumber from downed trees to build the Martha-Mary Chapel on the grounds of the Wayside Inn in Sudbury. Ford had bought the historic Longfellow's Wayside Inn in Sudbury, established a high school for boys, moved the Mary Little Lamb School to the property and built a gristmill. He had planned to build a historical village in Sudbury but instead built Greenfield Village, near Detroit, that included two or three old Sudbury houses. The Wayside Inn, schoolhouse, gristmill and chapel remain on the property in Sudbury.

FIRST GRADE CRISIS

One morning a CRISIS arose. Mom informed me—I could barely stand it—that there were NO clean underpants for me to wear. Had any boy ever survived such an event?

To my mind, there were two easy solutions:

1) Wear a dirty pair

or

2) Don't wear any at all

However, Mom came up with another. Wear a pair of my sister's BLOOMERS! I think I started to cry. Bloomers wouldn't be right at all as I stood in front of the urinal after recess.

If I hadn't cried on the school bus, no one would have known. Instead there were questions, "Why are you crying?" I can't remember what happened. Up to now I had put it completely out of my mind!

SCHOOL PUNISHMENTS

We behaved or else!

The longer I was at school, the more I learned about various punishments that were designed to help me behave.

The easiest was standing in the corner. You had to look straight into the corner and not get caught peeking out to see which buddy was laughing at you. Next on the list was standing in the corner where the wastebasket was—IN the wastebasket because you were trash. We were modern in one way, we didn't have a three-legged stool and a dunce cap.

We might be sent out to the hall or, for more serious punishment, to the cloakroom, where we put our lunches. We could secretly nibble on our lunch, but Mrs. J. was listening for any lunch box or wax paper noise. Not good to be caught!

We avoided notes home at all costs. Alan Flynn got a note that he was entrusted to take home. His father, Alan Flynn Sr., was principal of the town high school. On the way home on the bus, Alan thought the best solution was to open the window and let the note go. I remember watching it floating in the breeze. I'd like to know the outcome.

We had a reading circle just before lunch. If you needed extra reading help, you went up to the teacher's desk. I was at her desk waiting my turn, and the boy next to me must have said or done something bad because Mrs. J. swung her arm and slapped him on the lips. The problem is that her arm kept going and also slapped poor innocent me. It was a stinger! I wanted to save that slap, file it away for when I needed it. It didn't end up that way.

You would think that as I went to school I would get smarter, but no. There were to be two more punishments, but not until fourth grade. Miss Hemingway taught third and fourth grades in the other large classroom. HINT: These punishments-to-come were NOT standing in the corner.

MY FRIEND ROGER

Roger MacArthur was my best friend. He started first grade at South School a year before I did. He didn't pass first grade that year, so we became classmates. He was a year older, and the important part was that he was bigger and tougher.

Roger was one of five children and had two older sisters and two brothers. They grew up in Sudbury with his Uncle Martin and Aunt Linda Strand, who owned a large chicken farm.

Aunt Linda worked in Boston with Dr. Frank Lahey as the #2 person at the Lahey Clinic. There was a mysterious concrete building at the farm, sort of like a bomb shelter, that held all the Lahey medical records. No computers then.

The only person Roger was afraid of was Aunt Linda. However, that didn't stop Roger in any fashion. His only comment was, "My Aunt Linda will kill me." So I suppose it was enough that he should be concerned.

In the first grade, it was like having the Mafia on my side. Once some bigger kids were bothering me. Roger came by and put a stop to that! If they bothered me, they bothered Roger. Meeting bullies in first grade was new for me.

I was in the doghouse more often than Nancy.
But when it came to moving across the road,
although I was too little to be much help
I remember being excited about the move.
It included borrowing a big truck from the pig
farm to move our wooden mink houses
on skids across the road with the
mink still in their pens.

MOVING ACROSS THE ROAD
Spring 1939

I was surprised to learn that we now owned the empty and forlorn house across the road. My father had bought the house and nine acres from the bank.

Some improvements came before we moved. The first order of business was lighting numerous special candles to fumigate the house. We (parents) cleaned and painted everything inside. Outside, Dad covered over the dump and planted a new lawn.

After the serious cleaning, we moved household, pets and mink across the road. Our two pigs were afraid to cross the road and balked. A large truck pulled the wooden mink houses—holding breeding stock—on skids across the street and got stuck.

Our new house with Nancy and me in the foreground and Dad and Mom standing near the front porch. This photo was taken after the front yard dump was covered and graded and before the lawn was planted.

JOHNSON FAMILY NEIGHBORS

Next to us up the street lived the Johnson family: Nels (Nelsie) and Marie and their six children. I knew and loved them all.

Daughters Edith and Elsa were married and lived in Sherborn and Framingham. Eric had grown up and moved away.

Next was Ed who worked at Boston Supply, a hardware store in Framingham, the town where we shopped. It seemed like a city to me. I would always stop in to see him and get a joyful greeting. He always asked what was going on in Sudbury.

Elmer (Elmie) and Carl (Kelly), bachelors in their early 20's, still lived at home. They both worked for my father at Philgas. They often dropped in at our house and always teased Nancy and me.

Nels was like a grandfather to me. He was always glad to see me. I would walk with him down his grassy lane to the pasture to get the cows in the afternoon and drive them back to the barn for end of day milking. At other times, I would ride with him on a wagon or watch him doing the evening chores. I never knew details about his coming from Sweden nor when he and Marie had married.

THE COWS & THEIR BARN

I loved visiting in the barn. The barn was fun with Nels milking the two or three cows, fewer than there had been in its heyday when he was young. Oftentimes there might be a newborn calf in the calf pen. Calves always wanted to suck a couple of fingers if you offered. They were so cute. The barn cats would come around at this time to share a saucer of fresh, warm milk. Nels would sit on a three-legged milking stool, lean his head on the cow's flank and sort of sing a soft melody. There was a bench behind the cows that I would sit on and watch him milk. The cats would come and watch and hope for a squirt of milk.

After milking, the milk was filtered into a stainless steel pail in the milk house and submerged in a tank of cold water. The overflow of this water ran into the watering trough for both the horses and the cows.

In front of the tie-ups was a large grain bin. I would often pick out hard corn kernels from the bin to chew. The main part of the barn held the hay. Nancy and I would jump in the hay and build tunnels. The middle of the barn held wagons. A tool room was at one end under part of the haymow. The door at the end was very heavy and moved on little iron wheels. It was opened in the spring and closed in the fall.

THE WORK HORSES & BROWNIE

Another building was a horse stable, and it was fun to watch the horses. I would go into one of the stalls but not the other one—that horse kicked. I don't know why the horse stable was set apart from the cow barn.

The horses had a busy life: hauling manure from under the cow barn and plowing in the spring; cultivating corn and hauling hay in the summer. It was fun to ride atop the high loads of hay. In the fall, they might haul a load of logs bound for the saw mill or a load of apples to the cider mill. Later, during the winter when the ground was frozen, on the heavy sledge they'd bring in loads of firewood from the wood lot.

The barnyard was fenced off between the cow barn, the horse stable and the milk house.

Brownie was their large bird dog, usually quite lonely. He lived in a large doghouse. To escape the cold winter winds, Brownie sometimes invited me into his house where his bed was a snug circle made of hay.

The Johnsons' pig was Wally. He was named after Wallace Simpson. King Edward VIII abdicated the English throne in 1936 in order that he could marry the divorced Mrs. Wallace Simpson—quite the scandal at the time. Here I am with Bobby and Wally.

OTHER FARM MEMORIES

When I was very young, one day I saw a "VERY LARGE killer snake" at the farm. In retrospect it was probably a small garter snake. I "escaped" onto a lumber pile and started bawling my head off. Mrs. Johnson finally "saved my life" by outwitting the snake and setting me free.

Once in the cow pasture, barefoot—almost always—I came up with a new skill. I ran to see how far I could slide on the fresh cow flops. My mother was not impressed. This is not going to be an Olympic sport!

One of my favorite books was *The Adventures of Jimmy Skunk*, written by Thornton W. Burgess. Another book in the series was *The Adventures of Reddy Fox*. The little folks of the Green Forest and Green Meadows often dealt with the Brown Farm and farmer Brown's boy. In my little world, I compared Nels Johnson's farm to Farmer Brown's farm and made up my own stories. The chicken house was sturdy and well built. Jimmy Skunk and Unc' Billie Possum could not get into the Johnsons' chicken coop, a busy, bustling place. Outside the coop was the chicken yard, built out of strong wire netting and so well built that Reddy Fox could not get into the yard. Later in my adventure story, I imagined that I was in the same predicament as Reddy Fox.

Nels raised and sold asparagus. He had a really neat old table/bench that was set up to make tidy bunches of asparagus. When he had too much to sell, he would ask me to take some home to my mother. My polite reply was, "No, thank you." At the supper table at home, I would have to eat some of everything, but I didn't have to eat anything that wasn't there. Years later, Mom found out about my refusals. She was well put out to realize what had gone on—and all the delicious fresh asparagus my family had missed.

Sunday afternoons at the Johnsons' were big get-togethers. Their kitchen was hot with coffee on the large wood-burning stove, tasty treats from the Swedish bakery and plenty of noisy people. I would get a little coffee so as to be able to dunk a hard rusk treat.

Dottie Fredrickson, one of the Johnsons' cousins, often came out from Boston for a day's visit. She was a nurse and worked with Sister Kenney, who was famous for working with polio patients in iron lungs before the polio vaccine was developed. Dottie always had a fairly new Chevrolet convertible and took us kids on rides. What fun!

29

THE GENTILE FAMILY NEIGHBORS

The Gentiles, truck gardeners on Coolidge Lane behind the mink sheds, were neighbors with nine sons: Joe, Jimmy, twins Patsy and Frankie, Geno (Squeaky), Salvatore (Sussa), Tony, Danny and a baby brother.

They farmed their land and also some of our land, which was beautiful black river-bottom loam. One year they raised tomatoes, and I carried a little saltshaker around with me as I helped myself to misfits, but not to the #1's destined for the Boston market. Nancy and I were tasting sweet peppers once and by mistake got into the **HOT** ones. I can still taste them!

One day some of the Gentiles' friends visited from Boston. We saw a woman catch a chicken, wring its neck and hide it under her coat. We told Mr. Gentile what we had seen. We thought we were quite the detectives. But Mr. Gentile said it was O.K., maybe she needed the chicken more than he did.

Past their house were a house, a barn and a well-house, all of which had seen better days. The main part of the house was used for raising chickens. That gave it a few more years of useful life. On the other end was an ell, probably originally used as a kitchen. The ell was falling down, but was still a snug, fairly warm abode for an old gentleman named Joe Vaccaro. I never knew where he came from or where he went, but it was another place we could drop in to visit, and he was interesting. His room was quite small. We saw a small Glenwood kitchen stove for cooking and heating, a small bed and a couple of chairs.

DAD & THE GENTILES' TRACTOR

My father grew up on a farm in Iowa *before there were tractors or trucks.* One day he wanted to use the Gentiles' tractor that was parked in their garage. It was an old Ford with steel wheels, *before the time of three-point hitches,* and it started by a hand crank. If you hit a root or rock when plowing, it would rear up in the air and could turn over backwards and upside down. Those Ford tractors were known as "man killers."

One day Dad could not get it started. By mistake, he left it in gear. Later, Jimmy Gentile got it started and, still in gear, it went right through the back of the garage and into the chicken yard. Jimmy jumped out of the way just in time and, thinking it was his fault, ran away. We were all worried, so went looking for him. To everyone's relief, he came back late that evening.

When I was in fifth grade, the Gentiles moved away. My best pal, Geno, was gone. I missed him. At that stage of your life, you think you will never get over it.

Much later, John White became my accountant. John specialized in farms and had clients who were mink farmers, carnation growers, rose growers and such. He brought me up-to-date with Geno, who by then owned a greenhouse and was happily married.

BLUEBERRIES &
HOP BROOK ADVENTURES

Farther back along a path at the end of Coolidge Lane was a wonderful big patch of wild high-bush blueberries loaded with berries in July—good picking for us and our neighbors. Mom's blueberry pies were the BEST!

On the other side of Coolidge Lane, Landham or Hop Brook meandered toward the Sudbury River. Back in earlier times, the brook was part of a meadow that produced a valuable hay crop. Then farther downstream, somewhere in Billerica, they dammed the river. The water backed up, changing a nice hay meadow into more of a swamp.

The brook was our hot weather spot where we swam and played on a homemade raft. As we boys approached the swimming hole, we stripped off our shirts—if we were even wearing them—and shorts. Part of the routine was to swim across the brook, dry off and plaster ourselves from head to foot with mud. Then a quick naked dip and back to normal. Once in a while girls yelled before they arrived, giving us time to put our shorts back on.

One day my buddy "Squeaky" and a couple of other Gentile boys were walking along Coolidge Lane and met three other boys, strangers. We asked who they were. They said they were from Waltham. Home of the Waltham Watch Company, Waltham was 10 or 12 miles toward Boston on Route 20. They said they had ridden up on the bus. Anyway, we didn't like them in our territory, so we were yelling back and forth until this encounter ended with a rock fight.

We were on a gravel lane with plenty of ammunition on both sides. If you ever get in a rock fight, you can't dodge rocks quick enough. So, take off your coat and hold it in front of you. When a rock comes toward you, let the rock hit your coat and fall harmlessly in front of you. Then throw it back. The interlopers finally went back where they belonged. Turns out they had broken into Joe Vaccaro's little hovel.

After relating this adventure to the grownups, we decided to contact Seneca Hall. This was big time! Seneca Hall was the Sudbury constable. There were no Sudbury police at that time. Seneca had a 1937 Ford to carry him in pursuit of his duties. He was part Seneca Indian, but I'm not sure what part. We wanted the Waltham boys prosecuted to the full extent of the law, but the results have faded away in my memory.

We always had something to do, or if we didn't, it was not for long.

Two of the Gentiles' cows once went loose and up-town by the library, so someone had to get them and lead them home. The usual way to town was to go up Landham Road to Route 20 and then west to South Sudbury village. A shorter way, which the cows took, was across the brook and across the swampy meadow, over the railroad tracks and into town.

We took the shorter way and caught the cows in no time at all. I don't remember which Gentiles were with me, but I ended up leading the second cow. The first cow left a patty cake on the road. The cow I was leading stepped in it and then immediately stepped on my bare foot. What luck! Because her hoof was cow-pie slippery, it slid right off and didn't hurt a bit. I don't remember the rest of the trip, but we knew where to ford the brook and got the cows back to the Gentiles' barn. That was enough excitement for that day.

The barn wasn't too exciting on my mental list of Places to Go & Things to Do, but an interesting place was the well house nearby. There was no pump. All the water for the cows and chickens came up the well by hand, using a pail and rope.

Maybe the cows had run away because they wanted to be town cows with fancier modern perks.

33

THE CUTLER FAMILY NEIGHBORS

When I was six and seven, my horizons expanded. Beyond the Johnsons were the Cutlers: Mr. Roland Cutler and Mrs. Mary Goodnow Cutler and their six children, Isadore, Roland, Richard, Edward, Phil and Joe.

Mr. Cutler had been in an automobile accident and lost a leg. Almost every day he walked on crutches over a mile to the post office on Route 20 in South Sudbury and back. Young Joe drowned one winter while skating on Herds Pond.

Mrs. "Granny" Cutler was a Goodnow, a prominent Sudbury family. An early local library was founded by her family and named Goodnow Library. I loved the children's room and learned about penguins and so many other new facts. There was an Indian skeleton—*since removed*—and all sorts of Indian relics, arrowheads and local Indian pictures.

The Goodnow farm, now the Cutler farm, was King's Grant land from Colonial times, long before the American Revolution. I never met the king, but the huge barn was one of my domains.

I was fascinated with a how long a team of very large Percheron horses could pee. I wasn't done with the basics. There were tie-ups for cows, but the cows were long gone. I liked cranking the old dusty cider mill, apples or no apples. Old barns are scary when you climb up on the hay mow.

Out back was a spring house, and on a hot summer day nothing better than a cool drink of water. Out in the woods was a HUGE beech tree with all sorts of carved hearts and initials from long-gone generations. Next on the Cutler tour was the loveliest apple orchard… apples right off the tree— YUM! The sand pit came next with the best-feeling beach-like sand. The sand clumped in my hand, which was ideal for constructing roads and buildings in my play town. An added bonus was digging up snakes' eggs.

Next was riding in my car—the Cutlers didn't know it was my car. An old Ford Model A Phaeton that had seen better days had been retired into an old shed away from the house and barn. I sat in it and seemingly drove for hours. It never dawned on me that I should stop and gas up.

THE COW HORN

Dad had a horn, an old cow horn. *I still have it.* We called it the dog horn. He used it when hunting to call the dogs. By the end of the afternoon I might hear the dog horn. The sound carried for half a mile or more. When I heard that, I knew I was late getting home, which meant trouble. And I might have to dry the supper dishes. *This was long before the days of dishwashers.*

Sister Nancy was always home on time. Boring! Why did they have to always pick on me!

Dad would hunt foxes on moonlight winter nights, sometimes at the end of Stock Farm Road. His dog Duke might be miles away over the snow—beyond dog-horn reach—when Dad was ready to go home. So he'd take his hunting coat off and leave it on the ground by the Old Birch Gate. Early the next morning Duke would be there, waiting for a ride home.

I was probably seven or eight, holding Ginger and Snowball here on the lawn, with my first home in the background.

GRANDPARENTS & A GOAT

Grampa and Gramma Poole came to visit us again, this time by train, and stayed for a lengthy time. We drove to Worcester to pick them up when they arrived. Later Kelly Johnson and Jimmy Mercury wanted to travel, so they decided to go to Iowa and visit my Poole grandparents.

Dad asked them to be on the lookout to buy a couple of mink if the chance arose. Kelly was a big tease and wrote back that he was sending a goat. Dad thought he really meant a mink. But sure enough, about a week later there was a telephone call to Sudbury 204—our phone—from the Railway Express Office in Framingham to come and pick up our goat!

What a thrill for me to get a small Toggenburg goat. I named her Ginger and went to Nelsie's to borrow a cow chain to chain her out to graze. In no time at all, I was back at Nelsie's with a broken chain. He couldn't believe that his chains could hold the cows but could not hold Ginger. She broke more than one chain.

When Kelly arrived back from Iowa, he built a nice little goat house for Ginger on the back of the garage. That winter when she wouldn't drink much water, I offered her WARM drinking water. That was just what she wanted.

Ginger's first kids were twins, followed by quadruplets the following year!

Toggenburgs are a Swiss breed that absolutely love to climb. Ginger, whenever given the chance, would jump up on a car fender, next up on the hood and finally up on the roof. One time she fell through the canvas top of an insurance customer's car. Once she got into the house, jumped up on the table and dented our silver sugar bowl. From then on we had a crooked sugar bowl.

37

OLD NED

During the 1938 hurricane most of the pine trees in the woods at Lester Smith's mink ranch blew down. In January and February there is not much work to maintain the breeder herd of mink, therefore we had time to go logging. *This was before the time of chain saws and skidders.* It was two-man saws and, best of all, my introduction to Old Ned.

Ned was a LARGE workhorse that belonged to a mink farmer in nearby Wayland named Tewksbury. He was an old fashioned skidder, blind in one eye and hard of hearing. He pulled logs out of the woods to where they could be loaded on a truck for the journey to the sawmill. As the logging progressed there were trails created all through the woods. Ned would start off pulling a log and if you could yell "gee" loud enough he would go right or "haw" he would go left. After he had gone on a trail a couple of times he could follow it alone.

At the end of each day I rode him a third of a mile to the barn where he stayed. One day on the way home he saw a team of horses and started running toward them full speed ahead. As a workhorse, he was wide and didn't have a saddle so my legs went straight out to each side. I couldn't stop him nor slow him down till he got to the team, but I was still holding on so was able to head him again to the barn.

When the logging for the year was done, logs were trucked to the sawmill and I was appointed to ride Ned over the back roads to Wayland. After six or seven miles of slow plodding. I needed to get off to stretch my legs and walk a bit. That was a good change, but how to get back on? I couldn't find any way. I walked. At last we were at Tewksburys'. Ned was home. The sawn logs were soon milled into boards ready to be cut into parts for more nest boxes for the mink.

LANDHAM ROAD PASSERS-BY

Although there was very little traffic on Landham Road when I was young, occasionally something showy passed by.

Once a year members of the Millwood Hunt Club rode by on handsome horses—a thrill to watch. About two dozen riders wore colorful red-and-white riding and hunting apparel. A pack of unleashed tri-color hound dogs followed.

Every spring a fancy coach drawn by four white horses toured all the towns in the area. A man on top blew a horn to alert people in the houses. The coach advertised the Red Coach Grill, a restaurant on the Wayland-Weston line. The restaurant was closed all winter, and the coach and horses announced the spring reopening. The rest of the year the coach was on display on a large pedestal outside the grill.

FOURTH OF JULY

After the annual Fourth of July parade from South Sudbury to Sudbury Center with soldiers, scouts, bands, floats and fire trucks, the volunteer firemen put on an outdoor fair/carnival at the high school. A band performed on the band stand, Bingo was popular, and there was glorious fair food. Of several booths, one is burned into my memory—a sign of the time. A small tent set back aways with a hole cut in the canvas. Up front three baseballs were sold for a chance to "Hit the Nigger on the Head."The last thing at night was a huge bonfire and fireworks display.

I still wish that my birthday were July 4.

SUDBURY SCHOOLS

REPORT OF *James Poole* .... GRADE *1*

September to January	Reading Satisfactory Number work Satisfactory Spelling Satisfactory Writing Satisfactory	Promotion prospect Good
January to April	Reading Satisfactory Number work Satisfactory Spelling Satisfactory Writing Satisfactory	Promotion prospect Excellent
April and May	Reading Satisfactory Number work Satisfactory Spelling Satisfactory Writing Satisfactory	Promotion prospect Will be promoted

Pupil is promoted to Grade *II* .... Teacher *Sarah M. Johnson*

I was a satisfactory student in first grade (above),
but before spring in second grade (below) Mrs. J. noted,
"more effort needed," which became a recurrent
note in my school career.

SUDBURY SCHOOLS

REPORT OF *James E. Poole* .... GRADE *2*

September to January	Reading S Number work S Spelling S Writing S	Promotion prospect Excellent
January to April	Reading S Number work F (more effort needed) Spelling S Writing S	Promotion prospect Good
April and May	Reading S Number work S Spelling S Writing S	Promotion prospect Excellent

S - Satisfactory

Pupil is promoted to Grade *3* .... Teacher *Sarah M. Johnson*

JUNK DEALERS

In the late 1930's there was increased activity by junk dealers throughout farming communities. This was near the end of the Great Depression, and people were glad to change scrap metal into cash. This scrap metal was sent by boatload to Japan. Their island nation was and is quite short on natural resources. Scrap metal was valuable. Turns out the Japanese were building up their war effort.

ME, A GERM

Once in second grade I was given the part of a germ in a health play. It entailed dancing with a girl. This worried me! At the last minute, I was saved. Because I was a germ, I got sick and stayed home.

TO WRAP UP FIRST & SECOND GRADE

They thought I was smart because of my sister Nancy's trailblazing record. I was "satisfactory" in first grade. But by second grade and many grades beyond, I fooled them. I tended to be lazy: "...more effort needed."

Unlike Nancy, when first grade was half done, guess what? I wasn't promoted across the room to second grade! Not until after a full year of first grade was I "promoted to Grade II," but at the end of second grade, as you can see in my report card, I was "promoted to Grade 3"!

An infamous paper punch...

THIRD & FOURTH GRADES
fall 1940–summer 1942

SOUTH SCHOOL AGAIN

My third grade teacher was Miss Heminway.

Third grade went pretty well with satisfactory reports that noted, "if James tried a little harder his work could be excellent" and, "he cold do neater seatwork if he would try."

I don't remember the circumstances, but eventually Miss H. told me I could be kept after school if I didn't shape up. I wasn't worried about after school, but she lived past my house on Landham Road, and I would have to walk home with her.

That threat straightened me out quick.

NOT ALWAYS BAD

The following fourth grade stories may sound like I was always bad. That's not true, but try and write a story of me sitting in class day after day being good and see how many people want to read it.

All of a sudden summer was over. Instead of being free and outside, I was back in school and chained to a desk. I was in the third and fourth grade room with Miss H.—same teacher, same room.

Now I was bigger and older, so it was easier to get into more trouble.

43

IRVING'S PAPER PUNCH

After working all summer and being busy, I became bored. One day Irving Fay was absent. I decided to sit at his desk. After exploring all his things, I came upon his paper punch. This was right up my alley.

Even in third grade I was building nest boxes for the mink with a hammer and nails and real lumber. I looked all through Irving's desk but couldn't find any loose paper. Without thinking and still wanting to try the paper punch, I tried it out on a book. Everything in my life was still fine.

A few days later, Irving was back, I was at my desk, AND THEN... Irving discovered punch holes in his book. No one had ever been murdered at South School, but the investigation that ensued was worthy of one. Then the mystery was solved, and I was the culprit.

When the dust cleared and the sting of Miss H.'s ruler on my hand subsided, I was slated to appear not before the Principal, Mrs. Johnson, but—this was big time—before the SUPERINTENDENT, Mr. Benedict. In the comic strips once in a while a character walks around with a dark cloud over his head... that was me. Mr. B. only came once every few weeks. He had 12 grades at the Center School and all of Wayland Schools, so there I was, waiting...

Finally the day came. It was one on one: Mr. Benedict and me out in the hall.

Would it be the death sentence?

No. He was nice to me.

He understood that:

#1. I had not planned to do a dastardly deed.

#2. I had suffered by having to wait to meet with him.

#3. He knew I would never do anything like that again.

#4. I was free, free at last.

The rest of my life he was my real hero.

SNOWBALLS

Another early life-learning experience involved snowballs. **DON'T** throw snowballs. **DON'T** throw snowballs. Phyllis Ann Phelps squealed on me.

"Tattle tale, tattle tale, sitting on the bull's tail, when the bull begins to pee, you shall have a cup of tea."

There were four or five of us on the fourth grade "throwing snowballs" list. The punishment was over Mrs. J.'s lap for a hard spanking in the furnace room.

Here is where I made the wrong decision. I got at the front of the line to get it over with. That happened, but Mrs. J. was fresh and strong. As the back of the line got nearer she was breathing harder and harder, and the spankings got lighter and lighter.

Feeding the mink in the outside pens was my job.
My gloves were too big for my hands, but I had to make do.
Note the watering cup attached to the end of the wire pen.
At the other end of the wire cage was an entrance hole cut
into a pine box that provided cover from inclement weather.
A hinged door on the box permitted access by workers.

FEEDING THE MINK

Soon after moving across the road and before the war, feeding about 1,000 mink in separate pens all summer and fall kept us busy. I was in charge of feeding five rows. All the food was raw. In the summer we fed them late so the heat of the day wouldn't spoil the food. A dog or a fox can eat spoiled food, but if a mink ate spoiled food it would die of food poisoning.

We fed a balanced diet with different percentages according to the time of year: 30% fish, 25% beef by-products, 20% chicken or duck by-products, 20% grain and 5% miscellaneous, which would include milk, cod liver oil, wheat germ oil, brewers yeast, tomalfa (which was moist and came in a heavy oak barrel) and alfalfa leaf meal (so dusty that we ran out of the feed room after dumping a pail-full in the mixer).

Once when the weather was cold I remember pushing a wheelbarrow of feed from the mixer up the steep icy ramp. My feet slipped back, I lost my balance and my face smacked into the middle of the load of cold, mushy, fishy feed.

TAKING PELTS TO NEW YORK CITY

Pelting time was in late November. The mink that would be turned into luxurious fur garments were killed, skinned, fleshed and dried before they were packed up to be shipped to Hudson's Bay Company in New York City.

I was in fourth grade the first time I went to New York. Nancy and I were woken up early and asked if we would like to travel to New York City. We would be taking all the pelts in the car instead of shipping them via Railway Express. It was odd to see the whole year's work in a few cardboard shipping containers.

We went on the Merritt Parkway, a fairly new road leading through a corner of Connecticut into Westchester County, New York. Every bridge on the parkway was designed differently. Adjoining New York parkways led into the metropolis, where Nancy, Mom and I toured the city. On Fifth Avenue we rode on a double-decker bus. It was a treat. I don't remember most of what we did but it was a long day—we went from Sudbury to the city and back home in one day, 210 miles each way.

The day was important for Dad. He saw what other ranchers were producing and which skins were bringing the highest prices at auction.

OUR DAY OFF

By spring we fourth grade students had worked so hard that we thought that we deserved a day off. The school didn't offer one, so my pal Don Kiefer and I took one. At the morning bus stop I said I was going to Don's bus stop, and he said he was going to my bus stop. That meant we met in between stops.

Off to the woods for the day!

We had our lunches in paper bags. We also had a Boy Scout First Aid Kit. It had Hazoline tablets so we could drink bad water and survive. Time didn't pass as fast as we thought it might. We heard the noontime siren and started to get bored.

Eventually we headed for home. My father wondered what we were doing home. He thought we had been at school and had left early. He wanted us to go back to school. We explained that we had never been to school so couldn't go back for just one hour. Dad said if I didn't want to go to school maybe I would rather work making nest boxes for the mink. I didn't mind this, but not for long stretches in a row.

Next day while in line in the basement, Mrs. J. gave a long lecture on skipping school. We knew who she was talking about but she never mentioned any names.

ROAD REPAIR

Fixing the road in summer was exciting. I'd be barefoot, watching and wandering about as a large tank truck filled with liquid hot tar sprayed a thin coat on the road. Next came small local dump trucks hauling sand that they spread on the oil. The town hired these trucks as needed and also used them for plowing snow in winter. Kids hanging around could usually get a ride. *Try that today!* The joy of road repair was lost a bit when I returned home with tar on my bare feet. Mom was not pleased. My world was not perfect, but I felt blessed.

Near the gas station where Landham Road began, the railroad passed under a bridge. The road went up the hill to the wooden bridge. A sign read, "10 TON LIMIT." The town owned an old steamroller. It was heavy and slow— eventually a gasoline engine replaced the steam engine. To finish the road repair the roller had to go over the railroad bridge. Remember the 10-Ton Limit? Ally Noyes got off the roller near the top of the hill and watched it go slowly over the bridge all by itself. Then he quickly walked over the bridge, got back on and rode down Landham Road.

A SHARED BICYCLE

Nancy and I shared a girls' bicycle. It was a used bike that had cost five dollars. I don't remember fights over whose turn it was to use, but I did get into trouble. Nancy's friend Alice Chamberlain came one day on her bike. While they were playing, I took her bike and returned long after it was time for her to go home. That was trouble. She had to go home without it. On the bike I had been able to find unfamiliar territory.

All great explorers have to start somewhere.

BICYCLES NO LONGER SHARED

Nancy and I outgrew our sharing.

The next development was that Nancy bought a rebuilt girls' bicycle that was blue. Now I had a bike, the old one, all to myself.

Needless to say I was tough on it. One day, coming back down the hill from the gas station, I felt a thump, one of the bars had snapped and broken. I didn't want to walk home, so I got back on and another one snapped. This left only one bar holding the bike together. It held all the way home.

You may wonder why the disintegration. One day I had been on Coolidge Lane practicing jumps—over a short board balanced on a bushel box. This was boring after a while so I decided I would do the biggest ever. This was before Evel Knievel was ever heard of. FOUR bushel boxes piled up with the board ramp.

What was I thinking? That was the problem. I wasn't thinking at all. I went flying up in the air—that part was fine. When I came down the bike bounced into the ditch on one side and I went into the ditch on the other side.

Two skinned knees and two skinned elbows and my body shook up enough that I wouldn't try that again.

NEW BICYCLE FOR ME

Finally the day came for a trip to Landry's bicycle shop in Framingham. I had been saving money forever. I picked out a bright red Rollfast bicycle, a stripped down model. It cost $23. I had to borrow $2 from Mom to complete the deal.

Now I was approaching the big time!

THE BROOK AGAIN

Just down Landham Road was a three-arched stone bridge over the brook. It was built to last. Our favorite fishing hole was under the bridge. Nancy and I fished for hornpout, red perch and sunfish. One day Nancy pulled in a large sucker, a real surprise! It wasn't good to eat, but it was our largest catch. Another time, I caught a hornpout and put it in the freezer. When it thawed it was still alive. It wasn't a deep freeze.

One day Mom sent me to the post office. I didn't have a carrier on my bike, so I tucked all the mail inside my shirt. I knew it was important business mail, but what could go wrong? Almost home, I stopped at the bridge and leaned over the railing to watch the water. Pretty soon I was surprised to see an envelope float by, then another and another. All the mail was on a voyage out to sea. I hustled farther down to where the brook turned and got narrower. I found a long dead branch and with much agitation was able to recover all the mail. Try and explain soaking wet letters to Mom.

One summer I made a two-foot diameter undershot waterwheel. I was proud of my waterwheel. It made a fun plop, plop, plop, plop sound. I could stop, look and listen every time I passed by. It worked all summer, but after a large rainstorm it washed away.

CUT FOOT

One summer day I was barefoot, as usual, and rode my bicycle down Coolidge Lane near Gentiles' barn where Joe Vaccaro used to live. The area was abandoned and grown over in tall grass near where the old well house used to be. I was off the bike and walking around when "Oh!" I had stepped on the bottom half of a broken bottle. I knew it was a bad cut. I got back on my bike and started for home peddling with one foot. Reaching home I announced, "I am cut bad!"

The cut was on the outer edge of the middle of my foot. Dad, who usually played doctor, admitted that maybe it was bad enough for a real doctor. But things began to settle down and bandages were discussed. I heard Dad ask Mom if a Kotex pad was sterile. I didn't think I would like one on my foot. But even though it was my foot, I was not in charge.

Later my foot throbbed. I couldn't put any weight on it. I sat with my foot on a pillow on a footstool, and everyone answered my beck and call. At night even a light blanket was too heavy.

One of my favorite books by Thornton W. Burgess was *The Adventures of Reddy Fox*. Reddy had been warned time and time again about stealing chickens at Farmer Brown's. Reddy never listened and as a result got his foot shot by Farmer Brown's boy. Anyhow, Reddy spent days sitting on the doorstep outside Granny Fox's house sunning himself. I started to do the same.

I watched six or eight cars go by in the morning and back again at night. Little by little I could bear to touch my foot to the ground. At last one day, Dick Cutler arrived with a pair of crutches. What a relief. I could move around. It was three weeks before I could really walk again. I never knew how long it took Reddy to recover. But at least I didn't have Granny Fox giving me grief.

THE AMES FARM

An interesting spot was the Ames's farm farther down Landham Road. This was beyond my earlier territory, but I was now old enough to add it to my travels. It was a bigger farm with more cows and a bull. There was a spring on a nearby hill. It was always running and piped into the barnyard's watering trough. A collie dog helped manage the cows when they needed to be sent inside and the bull when he was let out. There also was a large apple orchard and an apple storage house with an elevator, which was an oddity to have in those days.

And then again, there was Nels Johnson, who would harness up one of his horses to a wagon and hitch a cow on back to be led to Ames to be bred. I'd get to ride along.

Citizens were encouraged to grow produce during the war. Potatoes were a cooperative effort among Pooles, Cutlers and Ames. A crew of wives cut up seed potatoes, leaving one eye on each piece. The Cutlers had an 8N Ford tractor and a potato planter; they planted. The Ames had an old potato digger that hitched to the 8N Ford, and I drove. Its special digger chain pulled potatoes out of the ground, shook the soil off them and piled them in a row. The chain often broke. Neighbors gathered the harvested potatoes into burlap bags that were trucked away to sell or stored in local cellars for winter use. Our Poole family ate 20 bushels of potatoes one winter.

In the spring the Ames's team of horses came by pulling a wagon. There were two cows in the wagon and another being led behind. Several trips took all the Ames's cows to a nearby meadow that would be their summer pasture.

SNAKES

One day I was barefoot and just walking along in that cow pasture when I felt something slippery. I had stepped on a long black snake that I saw a short time later swimming across the brook.

My dog Spotty loved to hunt frogs and snakes. If he caught a snake in his mouth, he would shake his head back and forth and kill it like cracking a whip. One day he found such a big snake he couldn't snap it back and forth. He could only shake a section at a time.

MERCURY'S GAS STATION

Mercury's gas station was on the corner where Landham Road ended at Route 20. It featured the big red Pegasus sign of Mobil Oil. Outside the station on one side was a grease pit. Cars then had to be greased every 1,000 miles. To work under a greasy, oil-dripping car, one needed a hat. Once in a while Jimmy Mercury would give me a real prize, a cheap grease hat.

The gas station—a full-service station where a fellow pumped gas, checked the oil, and washed the windshield—was the center of life. Perhaps like an old-time general store. Inside was a sales counter with all kinds of smoking paraphernalia, Hershey Bars, Milky Ways, gum, etc., and an ice chest, with an attached bottle opener, that held ice water and all sorts of soft drinks in glass bottles. Most cost a nickel. It was a special treat to have a nickel for a soda or a candy bar.

There was a rugged metal table inside where one could sit and see the gas pumps and play card games. Rummy games were often boisterous affairs involving small-time bets.

BIKE RIDES

One day I decided to ride my bike to Saxonville, about three miles away. I didn't realize that would take me out of my territory. So off I went.

A bigger guy stopped me and growled, "What are you doing here?" He didn't beat me up. But he didn't let me go until after he spit in my face.

Another time, later, I rode my bike all the way through Saxonville to Framingham, about six miles away. I was riding on the sidewalk, thinking that was safer than riding on the road. A policeman stopped me—the true young country-bumpkin—and explained that sidewalks were for pedestrians (walkers) and not bicyclers. Sudbury had no sidewalks, how was I to know? He let me go without a ticket or time in jail.

Mom would have wondered where I was.

CUB SCOUTS

Cub Scout meetings were held once a week after school at Mrs. Dorothy Palmer's house, an easy walk from South School. We were brainwashed that the blue uniform with the yellow kerchief was the ultimate. It was a big deal to go to J.C. Penny in Framingham to pick out the right size uniform, and the neckerchief with the slide was like dessert.

Going up the ladder to Wolf, Bear and Lion was cool when I was nine, 10 and 11. By the way, if you want a package tied up, I can do a good job because of what I learned in Cubs. However, as good as it was, if I could use the tractor to plow the field, that took precedence over Cub Scouts.

The next best thing was being 12 years old and moving up to join Boy Scouts.

MRS. PRIEST

Mrs. Virginia Priest was a widow who lived down near the Cutlers. She owned and ran an old folks home. I cleaned her basement once in a while. She also owned a good barn with a nice tall indoor rope swing that we could use.

Once on my travels I noticed that there were a few broken windows in the barn. It didn't seem fair that anyone else was breaking windows that I considered mine. Anyway, I hung around there and added a few broken ones to the scene.

A few days later, guess what? My worst fears. Yes, Dad was involved. A phone call from Mrs. Priest: I had been seen in the neighborhood of the crime scene. Like all good criminals, according to the Rev. Caroline Neighoff, I lied (everybody sins) and said I didn't do it. I didn't convince Dad. If I didn't do it, I must go down and talk to Mrs. Priest.

A little black cloud followed me around for a couple of days. Just before I had finally put off the visit as long as possible, Dad received another call. Normally calls were not good. This one was excellent! Mrs. Priest wanted to apologize for accusing me of breaking the windows. Seems her nephew, while visiting from Boston, had done the dastardly deed.

You can never trust those bad city kids!

HERDS POND

Herds Pond was two miles from home on the back road to Wayland. One day Don and I decided to ride our bikes there and rent a rowboat. Bad Idea. We got to playing and into a water fight, splashing each other with the oars, which were old and, I think, starting to rot. You guessed it, we ended up breaking an oar.

Our wrongdoing was hard to straighten out and pay for.

HAWAIIAN RELATIVES

My mother was the youngest child by many years in her family. Before she was born, her oldest brother, Clarence, went off to see the world and ended up in Hawaii. He worked on a steam dredge in Pearl Harbor. He wrote home to Waterloo, Iowa, that he had met a girl. Folks at home wanted him to send them a picture of his girlfriend, Anna. He never did because she was a native Hawaiian. In 1914 they were married. In 1915 Edwin, their first child, was born. In 1917 another son, my cousin Herbert, was born.

That same year, 1917, Uncle Clarence was enjoying a day off when some one came running to say the steam pressure on the dredge was out of control. Clarence ran to check out the problem and arrived just as it blew up, killing him.

This tragedy left Anna and the two little boys by themselves with no means of support. She left the island with the boys and traveled back to where she had grown up and had some family. This was near Hilo on the big island of Hawaii. We lost track of our Hawaiian relatives until Aunt Maud made contact with cousin Herbert during World War II.

During my childhood, children were not as informed of everything as they are nowadays. Imagine my surprise to learn during the war that I had Hawaiian cousins I had never heard of: Edwin Keliihoomallu Weatherwax, who was born May 4, 1915, and Herbert, his younger brother, who was serving in the U.S. Army *(see Pearl Harbor, next page)*.

When Edwin was 15 he was diagnosed with Hansen's disease, generally known as leprosy. Leprosy was not treatable and was thought to be contagious. Edwin was interned with other leprosy sufferers on Molokai in Kalaupapa, where he died at age 50.

Today leprosy is treatable and known not to be contagious.

PEARL HARBOR

On the other side of the world from us in the middle of the Pacific Ocean is Pearl Harbor on the Hawaiian Island of Oahu. The Japanese attack on Pearl Harbor on Sunday, December 7, 1941, stunned the nation. We heard the devastating news on the radio that Sunday afternoon.

President Franklin D. Roosevelt addressed Congress on Monday to request a declaration of war, "Yesterday, December seventh, 1941, a date that will live in infamy, the United States of America was suddenly and deliberately attacked by naval and air forces of the Empire of Japan." It was that day that World War II began for the United States.

At nine years old I imagined all sorts of scenarios, probably some of them close to reality. There are volumes of history that tell the war story, but let's start in our family.

My cousin Herbert was in the U.S. Army at Pearl Harbor. He saw the attacking planes and witnessed the severe damage to our military and naval forces.

Herbert was sent to the mainland for further training. It was at this time that Aunt Maud was able to search records and make contact with Herbert. She then followed his movements throughout the war. Herbert ended his war service in Belgium in the final major battle of the European conflict, the Battle of the Bulge. After the war, Herbert attended Coyne Electrical School in Chicago as part of the GI Bill of Rights. That prepared him for starting his own electrical contracting business on Oahu.

As Herbert approaches his 99th year, he continues to volunteer at the Arizona War Memorial at Pearl Harbor.

Elmer (Elmie) Johnson

ELMER (ELMIE) JOHNSON

An early memory was being close friends with one of Nels Johnson's sons, Elmer. He was a friend of Mom and Dad. In his early 20's, he stopped by our house often and, as mentioned earlier, teased Nancy and me—much to our delight!

Elmie owned an airplane that he kept at Marlborough airport. He would fly so close to our house that the landing wheels would touch our large maple tree. He practiced spins, spirals and all sorts of maneuvers. I rode with him to Boston in an open cockpit biplane when I was seven years old. We circled Logan airport and its one passenger terminal.

Soon after, one day the radio reported that Elmer Johnson was killed in an airplane accident. I refused to believe it and wondered if it could be a different Elmer Johnson. Dad went next door to tell Nels, Elmie's father who was in the cow barn milking cows, what had happened. Nels stamped his foot on the floor and said he knew that would happen.

I remember walking up the road and into the Johnsons' house, smelling all the flowers and the women's perfumes, then going into a separate room with Dad, who showed me my first dead person. It was Elmie, the friend who meant so much to Nancy and me. *I tear up as I write this.* The men gathered in the cow barn.

A couple of days later the school bus had to wait on the way home from school for what people said was the longest funeral procession up to that time in Sudbury.

*Dad in his real estate and insurance suit, me in uniform
with a big smile on my face, Mom and Nancy*

FIFTH & SIXTH GRADES
fall 1942–summer 1944

CENTER SCHOOL

My fifth grade teachers in my new-to-me school at Sudbury Center were first Miss Hinkley and then Mrs. Brison.

Things went smoothly all year.

SCHOOL BUS

My school bus picked up all the kids in my neighborhood, grade school through high school. First through fourth graders were dropped off at South School and the older ones taken to Center School where there were classes from first grade through high school seniors.

Sudbury was a large town—25 square miles—with several neighborhoods: North Sudbury, Pine Lakes, Wayside Inn, South Sudbury, Landham Road in East Sudbury, and Sudbury Center. Each neighborhood used to have an early school, but South School was almost the last one still in use.

Once in a while, a high school boy would get kicked off the bus for a misdemeanor. Then he'd sneak out back and ride home on the back bumper and trunk space of the bus.

In the back of the bus was a bench seat that was mounted to the floor on hinges. This could be tipped over when the bus was moving so you could see the road. I think the hole in the floor made it easy to maintain and oil the rear differential.

FIREWORKS

I had a few firecrackers, and I figured out a great way to use them. I picked out a telephone pole that was situated so that the spike holes for climbing were aimed up the street. I put a firecracker in the hole with the fuse hanging out. I found a round rock that fit tightly in the hole. I drove the rock in and lit the fuse. The rock blasted out and up the road 200 or 300 feet! No one was injured or killed, and nothing was damaged. Again, I was blessed.

BOY SCOUTS

One of the games we played at Boy Scouts was Murder Circle on the floor. I got kicked in the head and got a concussion. I wasn't feeling good, so Dad took me to Dr. Ferrucci for x-rays. On the way home, I said my stomach didn't feel good. Dad "Doctor" Poole pulled over to the side of the road and said, "Get out." Then, "Stick your finger down your throat." You know what happened. That is what cured me.

Another game was Cock Fight. Six or seven boys lined up on each side, and one from each side met in the middle. Holding one foot up, the object was to knock the opponent down. That done, the loser was out of the game, and another replaced him in the middle to try to knock the leader down. The game was over when one side had no more boys. Being tall, I was good at it.

The Boy Scouts had a cabin on Nobscot Mountain, where sometimes we went for a day or overnight. Nobody explained to me to bring your own food. I thought food was provided. I'm sure I was hungry. I don't remember what happened next, but it must have been bad because I have forgotten.

SCOUT CAMP

Mom and Dad sent me for a week to Boy Scout Camp Resolute in Bolton, Massachusetts. I didn't like camp, it was like being in the Army with KP duty. A bugle played reveille to wake up and taps to go to bed.

While there, Irving of paper-punch fame and I went on a 14-mile hike to pass a hiking requirement for First Class Scout. Being at camp we didn't know the territory, and we got lost. We were supposed to find a post office, showing that we had been to a certain location.

We were tired.

It rained.

We were soaked.

The Boy Scout motto is "Be Prepared."

We were not prepared, and we lay down to rest in the middle of the road in some puddle. Eventually we got back but were late for supper.

By the way, I was never an Eagle Scout.

DANCING LESSONS

I think it was sixth grade when we were sent to take dancing lessons from "Hollywood" Haynes at the Town Hall.

We learned the waltz, the polka, square dances and the grand march. Boys gathered on one side of the hall and girls on the other. Ladies' choice was fun with Claudia Fulton running across to ask me for a dance.

AIR RAID CENTER

Our house was designated an Air Raid Center. From time to time there were practice air raid drills. Roger's brother Benjamin and his cousin Herman Brown would arrive on their bikes ready for duty as messengers. They were older boy scouts.

Everything was blacked out nightly as if protecting from an actual raid, because any light would be a target. Everyone had blackout curtains. Dad, the air raid warden, went up past the Ames's farm to check for lights showing. He might stop cars because there was, quote, "a bomb crater in the road."

Rationing was in effect throughout the town. Each person received a ration book. Each vehicle was given an A, B, C or D sticker denoting the amount of gas allotted according to need by use. Meat, sugar and certain other foods, such as butter, were on the ration list. We were limited to one pair of shoes per year. We saved and turned in all kinds of fats. Fat was a component of munitions.

Picnics and card games were popular entertainment. *No television.* Much more visiting back and forth among neighbors. There were regular meetings of the Red Cross at the Cutlers' house. Ladies wrapped bandages. Everyone raised crops. Each family that could had a victory garden. I remember staying home from Cub Scouts to plow our field.

EFFORTS FOR WAR

As the war progressed, there were things done for the "war effort." In the cities people donated old aluminum pots and pans. They built up huge piles of aluminum to be used in building U.S. fighter planes and bombers. Many young men joined the armed services. If someone was in a military uniform and hitchhiking, people would always stop and give them a ride. Many women were working in the defense industry. There were posters about these women. One was named "Rosie the riveter." Rosie earned money but couldn't buy a car or a washing machine or other durable goods, but she could buy a mink coat or stole. Mink pelts rose in value. The problem was that all the young men were doing defense work or were drafted. There were not enough laborers available to raise more mink.

Even giving one's hair contributed to the effort. As I write this, I am looking at a framed document with a lock of hair in it, given mid-1942 to thank Anna "Wendy" Wahlers, age 8½ years old.

"A gift of her hair from which selection will be made for use in instruments serving our National Defense and for the requirements of Science and Industry." The hair that could be used had to be straight blond, untouched by chemicals, hot irons, waving machines, etc., and at least 14 inches long.

"By the above kind act, not only has the national need been facilitated but the fund of the USO and the Red Cross have been benefited, as the cash market value of all hair used is being paid into those patriotic and humanitarian societies."

—Division of Bendix Aviation Corporation

Fifteen years later, Wendy and I were married.

PRISONERS OF WAR

We used about a ton of grain every week at the mink farm. It was added to the mixer after all the meat had been ground. George was the delivery driver of Purina mink chow. Many of his customers were raising chickens for meat, others were raising them for eggs. The grain came in 100-pound cloth bags. Customers complained they were too heavy, resulting in a change to 50-pound heavy paper bags. Then, as it turned out, most people carried two bags at a time.

One day George showed up with a helper. He was a German prisoner of war. These prisoners were based at Cushing General Hospital in Framingham. I visited the hospital once. It was built just for the war casualties. The hallways were the longest I had ever seen. They were spotless, and I assumed they were all maintained by the prisoners. These prisoners had the best deal ever. They weren't behind barbed wire and weren't cold or being shot at. They did all sorts of chores at the veterans' hospital.

GOLD STARS & WOMEN

Whenever we rode around, which wasn't often because of the gas shortage, we would count stars in front windows. Blue was the color of the star that denoted a member of the family in the armed services. A gold star was for a soldier or sailor killed in action.

Women also served in all sorts of branches of the services. Some piloted planes from where they were manufactured to military destinations.

MRS. PALMER REPLACED
MISS SAUNDERS

My sixth grade teacher was Miss Saunders, who was not nice. Her idea of teaching was to assign something and sit back to take care of her fingernails. One day a few kids were making popping noises by putting their fingers in their mouths and pulling them out fast with a satisfying "Pop!" This was going on all over the room at "suitable" intervals.

"The next one who does that stays after school!"

My downfall, as usual, was the challenge. Guess who couldn't let that go by. Near the end of the school day, little by little I moved from one row to another closer and closer to the door. Finally I was out the door and down the stairs to the boys' room, which was off limits to women teachers. She knew I was there. One more step and she would have seen me around a corner. She checked the South Sudbury bus to no avail. I can imagine her state of mind. Teachers don't like to come in second.

Meanwhile I raced to a stop sign at the cross road, a five-minute run from the school. My bus came. It stopped. Charlie, the bus driver, opened the door. I climbed in the bus to freedom. Missing my job feeding a shed of mink would be far worse than what Miss Saunders could dole out.

I don't remember the aftermath. The mink got fed. But as for Miss Saunders and me, it must have been bad, because I am good at forgetting things that should be forgotten. Miss Saunders was soon gone.

Mrs. Palmer was next (another Mrs. Palmer, not my Cub Scout den mother). She was so nice, we did all we could to please her. Every once in a while our class came to a screeching halt when she'd just received a letter from her husband serving overseas in the Army. As she read those letters her face just glowed. We behaved.

LESTER SMITH & WWII

Lester Smith appeared on the scene in Sudbury when I was five or six years old. He started a mink farm up on Route 20 near the Wayland town line. With mink raising in common, he and Dad became close friends.

Lester lived in a cabin near his mink yard and rented his nearby house to a descendant of Oliver Wendell Holmes. Lester drove a fancy yellow 1936 Packard convertible with a Tampa, Florida, sign on the rear license plate that impressed Nancy and me.

His mink ranch was similar to ours in that it was slowly growing. Around 1940 he moved his mink down past our farm to Stock Farm Road, which allowed him to upgrade. He built three new sheds and no longer had any covered outside pens. Lester still lived on Route 20. Because his feed room was there, the Smith truck passed our house on a regular basis sometimes several times a day.

Poole Mink Farm was our name. Skyline Mink Ranch was Lester's. If anyone knows the difference between a farm and a ranch, please let me know.

Then the war years arrived, Lester and his younger brother Alan were both drafted into the Army. Ray, a hired man, was on the job full time. Alan was once home on leave and begged to be allowed to drive the truck when hauling feed from the feed room to the ranch. Alan was killed in action in France, the youngest in his battalion to be killed.

TENDING OUR MINK & LESTER'S

In 1943 things changed. Lester was serving as a truck driver in France. Skyline Mink Ranch mink numbers had been cut back. Fewer breeder mink were saved. Then Lester and Dad reached an agreement: All the feed for both Lester's ranch and our farm was gathered and prepared in our feed room.

That fall, Dad mixed all the feed and fed our mink while Nancy and I were at school. When we got off the school bus we changed clothes, had a snack and went to Smith's. My time was so valuable that instead of riding my bicycle a mile and a half to Smith's, I drove the truck. Dad and I fed, and Nancy watered. I was responsible for feeding the first shed. We were busy until November pelting time decreased the herd and relieved the pressure.

Besides Lester, many others were being drafted across the whole labor spectrum. As the war progressed older men, married men and others who had been passed over before were beginning to be called up in the draft.

Another part of the war effort was raising chickens: broilers at Smith's ranch. In July the mink litters were separated into individual pens. For a number of days the kits would chatter and cry in their own way, and the mother mink was furious and upset.

It so happened that a recently separated mother got loose. She got into the chicken yard and killed a chicken. After that she went on a rampage killing 25 or 30 birds that were not old enough to market. Mama mink killed them by biting the back of their heads. Usually a loose mink will run away, but not this time. When I ran to catch her, she was ready to take on the world and me. I didn't have to chase her. I nabbed her easily in my heavy mink catching gloves and put her back in her pen.

FEEDING SMITH MINK
THROUGH RECORD HEAVY SNOW

The Smith mink ranch was almost a mile down Landham Road and then half a mile on Stock Farm Road. Early in 1944 there was such deep and heavy snowfall we couldn't get to the ranch to feed the mink. Landham Road was plowed, but not Stock Farm Road.

After missing a feeding we waited as long as we dared and then put buckets of feed on a toboggan and started walking from Landham Road down Stock Farm Road. The snow was drifted in places, and wading through hip-high snow was difficult. We put in an SOS to LeRoy Hawes, the road commissioner, to see if the road could be plowed.

What a relief when the road department Caterpillar grader with a large V plow showed up. An earlier town road commissioner had asked the citizens at a town meeting to purchase the grader. It was needed to maintain and improve the roads as Sudbury's roads slowly changed from horse-and-buggy use to ever-faster automobiles and trucks. The pro grader group won the debate. The grader was the only machine that could push back such drifts of snow. It provided much needed and appreciated relief.

STATE POLICE

One day I was sick and in bed at home. The State Police cruiser was following the bus as it dropped off students. A state trooper asked Nancy if her brother was home. It was a shock for her, and she didn't know if I was home or not. The next thing I knew Mom was calling upstairs that someone wanted to see me. As it was time for the school bus, I thought it was one of my buddies. When a state trooper in full uniform stepped into my room I would have fallen over backwards except I was already lying down.

Up on Route 20 there was a Ford dealership, closed down and vacant. Because of the war, no new cars were available for civilians, and besides there was another Ford dealership three miles away in Wayland. Did I know anything about all the plate glass windows being broken at the Sudbury dealership?

What a shock! But it was real. I didn't know anything about it. Then he asked what other boys lived around this area.

My mother took over. She said the only one was Roger, "But he wouldn't do anything like that."

His Eddie Haskel persona saved him. Of course Eddie Haskel in Leave It to Beaver wouldn't be around on TV until many years later.

The big mystery: did Roger break the glass? It was never solved. I can't figure out why I was a suspect.

TO BOSTON WITH ROGER

One balmy spring morning Roger showed up on his bicycle. He thought it would be a good day to ride bikes to school. That sounded O.K., so I asked Nancy to take my lunch with her on the bus. My lunch got to school O.K. and sat on my desk. Roger meanwhile laid out his plans.

We rode up to Route 20, ditched the bikes in the woods and waited for the Boston & Worcester bus. This was big time: the B&W bus headed for the big city. Roger always had money, and this day was on him. Mr. Flynn, the principal, asked Nancy the usual questions about how my lunch got there but not me. Did my mother know? This was great. Nancy was innocent, but she got all the grilling.

We were 50 years before "Ferris Bueller's Day Off."

We arrived in Boston without a clue as to what we could do. A trip up a tall building was fun, but that didn't keep us going all day. We went into a White Tower hamburger joint, and when the guy in charge went out back Roger put a couple more hamburgers on the grill and we left. We heard that Revere Beach had a great amusement park. We got on a trolley car and ended up there. This was a school day morning so the rides were not operating. All we could do was look around. It was pretty sleazy. Roger found an open shooting gallery so he bought 25 shots for 25 cents. That went so fast that Roger asked if the man could load in more shots. They reached an agreement. The gun held 100 shots.

HEADING HOME

It was time to head back to Boston.

We met a boy on the trolley. He asked if we were playing hooky.

"Yes."

"How long?"

"Today."

"What about you?"

"Two weeks."

A woman riding with us asked why we weren't in school. I said our school burned down.

She said, "Oh, I read about it in the paper."

Now it was time to head back to the B&W terminal. It's a wonder we had enough money for the fares and weren't stranded like Charlie on the MTA.

Back to the real world.

We got our bikes from the woods and headed home.

Dad didn't let me down. "If you don't want to go to school maybe you would rather rake mink manure."

It is strange that days like that are remembered 70 years later but ordinary school days are not.

OTHER ADVENTURES WITH ROGER

EGGS * Have you ever been in an egg fight? If not, come with me to Roger's house. Go into the large chicken house that has a wicked smell of ammonia. Get your eggs, fill your pockets. Don't get all the eggs from one area, spread out so when they collect the eggs it won't look fishy... I got all my pockets full, and when Roger came up to me he crushed all the eggs in my front pockets.

BARN * Next we went in the large white barn to see the two riding horses, mostly ridden by Roger's older sister, June. Roger climbed up above the hay loft near the high point inside the barn. He had a large beach umbrella with him. The only way to see if it would be a good parachute was—yes, you guessed it—try it. He didn't break a leg, but I didn't see him try it again.

RIDING * Another day, Roger suggested we go horseback riding. That sounded like fun and different. We rode all the way to Sudbury Center. We got to see everything at a slow pace because most of the time the horses were walking. Also we discovered girls: Claudia, my first great love, lived in Sudbury Center. A fun visit, then back to the barn.

CLAY PIGEONS * We were walking through the woods near Dr. Wolback's place another day and came upon a strange looking wooden tower. We climbed the tower and discovered a couple of boxes of clay pigeons. Nearby was the "gun" for shooting them off. It wasn't really a gun but a spring-loaded skeet launcher. We placed a clay pigeon on the arm and set it off. It sailed out quite a way. We figured that with one of us standing off with a stick and the other launching clay pigeons it would be like playing baseball. We took turns. If we made a hit there was a nice smash like a small explosion. This machine was for practicing bird hunting, but it was more fun than baseball. I don't think Dr. Wolback had as much fun as we did.

FIGHTS * Roger and I were best friends, but that did not mean we didn't have tough fights. After all, that's what friends do. Once, close to home, he threw my bike over the causeway fence into the meadow. Another day we were on our way to Cub Scouts with our friend Don. It was shorter to go across the brook over a fallen tree to the meadow, but Don wouldn't cross on the tree. Roger and I were upset because we had to backtrack nearly to where we started in order to go uptown by the road.

Martha's school photo, first grade

BABY SISTER MARTHA LOUISE

It was a beautiful sunny day in early May, actually May 6, 1944. Dad and I were working together preparing some pens for the first litters of the season. Nancy came out to the mink sheds to announce that Mom had given birth to a little baby girl to add to our family. Both Mom and baby Martha Louise were doing fine.

My world was getting bigger, speeding up.
Roger and I had adventured in Boston.
Nancy and I had traveled to Iowa.
World War II was finally heading to a conclusion.
Daily life as a seventh grader was about to begin.

Me in seventh grade

*As a seventh grader, eighth
graders were a very big deal.
As an eighth grader, ninth
graders were the big deal.
Dances were always a big deal.*

SEVENTH & EIGHTH GRADES
fall 1944–summer 1946

CENTER SCHOOL, GRADE SEVEN

Seventh grade was a whole new ballgame. Our class had advanced to a home room on the second floor of Center School, up an important flight of stairs to classrooms high above the lower grades. We were the youngest class upstairs, and we had better not forget it. No longer did we have a single grade teacher; each subject was taught by a different teacher.

Miss Mahoney was our English teacher. I tried to figure out why I needed to know about ADVERBS. Us [We] boys sat in class hoping against hope that we wouldn't be called up to the chalkboard to answer Miss Mahoney's questions in front of the class. If we missed a summons to the board we could relax and enjoy ourselves at the expense of the one called and fidgeting at the board.

One day, still clear as crystal in my mind, it was Kenny Hooper at the board. Miss Mahoney's question was about, you guessed it, ADVERBS. With all the boys enjoying Kenny's dismay and unsuccess at answering her questions, Miss Mahoney announced that she could not figure out how Kenny could stand there with his bare face hanging out and tell her that "that" was an adverb.

Maybe that was what prompted her to announce at the end of the school year that she had decided to become a NUN.

WOUNDED AT NOON

One noontime Kenny and I were messing around inside when he grabbed my hand and pulled me off balance. He swung me around off my feet so that I ended up hitting my head on the chalkboard tray—right between my eyes.

After seeing the nurse I ended up with a bandage held on by a large and wide white adhesive tape "X" that was centered between my eyes. When I got off the school bus and into the house, I thought my mother was going to faint!

SATURDAY NIGHT DANCES

Starting in seventh grade there were Saturday night dances held in the Town Hall. Roger learned to play the clarinet and played in the band. Because it was still wartime, everyone stayed pretty close to home, and seventh graders were big shots on Saturday nights.

FORMAL DANCES

There were so few students in high school that students in the seventh and eighth grades were invited to take part in the junior prom and senior reception. Formal gowns, tickets, corsages—the whole works—and asking a girl.

MY FIRST DATE

We carried our lunches from home in brown paper bags and ate at our desks, then went outside to play. One day I had not gone out but was still eating and found myself alone with Claudia Fulton. This was the beginning of something grand that led to my asking her to the formal junior prom.

GETTING A CORSAGE

There was a greenhouse down the road from the school. Somehow I managed to order a corsage for Claudia to wear at the prom.

During school hours, we were not allowed off school property, but at noontime I sneaked out. I needed the corsage to stay in a cool place until dance time, so I picked up the corsage and kept going to Claudia's house a bit farther down the road. Gathering up all my nerve, I knocked on the door and explained to Mrs. Fulton that I'd like her to keep it cool until I picked Claudia up for the dance.

Claudia moved to Vermont in ninth grade.

THE LLOYDS

We hardly ever had a new student in our class (and rarely did one move away). But during the war, the Lloyd family moved to Sudbury. John and Richard Lloyd, who were twins, joined our seventh grade class. Their sister, Margaret, went to my sister's class, and their younger twin brothers went to a lower class. John and I became close friends.

Mr. Lloyd was in the British Army, and Mrs. Lloyd had connections to Sudbury. They chose to move to the U.S. from London, England, to get away from the German bombing.

After the war the Lloyds went back to England for a while but then ended up in the United States.

SOCCER

Fall was soccer season. We played at recess and at noontime. Sudbury soccer was played on a plain grass field with:

- *No set boundaries*
- *No official soccer ball*
- *No marked goals*
- *No uniforms*
- *No padding*
- *No timing*
- *No fouls*
- *No officials*

The only bell marked the time to return to classes.

One day the bell rang, and most everyone began to return to class. I don't know how it started, but it was West Sudbury versus East Sudbury, one on one, two boys who didn't like each other. One was me. I wasn't a bully, but I was sick of taking any more guff from Warren.

We grabbed each other and were rolling around on the grass and dirt—not good for school clothes. Five or 10 minutes after the bell, I showed up in class and he in his class. Seeing scrapes and dirty clothes, Roger wanted to know what happened.

"Warren gave up when I got a scissors hold on him."

Warren never bothered me again. It was worth it.

SOUTH SUDBURY

South Sudbury's metropolitan center was uptown on Route 20. There was a grocery store where Billy Pride fetched items you asked for, put them on the counter, penciled the cost of each item on a paper bag, totaled it as he bagged the groceries, took and rang up your cash (or put the total on your account), handed you the bag and thanked you.

Mr. Crowley's drug store was next door. He was grumpy and often spit on the floor. Somehow we survived, despite few health codes. The soda fountain was the major attraction. We liked to watch the pinball machine, but I never played. We never had anything to show for money we spent. For a nickel we could buy a Hoodsie, a small cup of ice cream made by the Hood Milk Company. There was a choice of flavors and a picture of a movie star under the lid.

A college ice was two or three scoops of ice cream topped by delicious hot chocolate. Roger ate three one day for his long walk home. A motorcycle came by, so just for fun he stuck out his thumb. He was a most surprised boy when the motorcycle stopped for him. It might have been that he had two older sisters. Another time Roger bought a bag of 100 BIG GOBS of Fleer's double bubble gum, a whole dollar's worth! It came wrapped in a cool wax paper comic strip.

Oh how I wish I could once again taste that gum.

THE COAL YARD & COAL

On the way home we went toward the coal yard next to the railroad. Coal came in on a coal car and unloaded by gravity down into a big pit to a conveyor belt that loaded a small dump truck for delivery to a home. The truck was weighed on a big set of scales because coal was ordered and sold by the ton. We were so interested in the coal yard that we forgot all about the gum and left the bag at the yard. We were far away when we remembered the 90 remaining pieces and just had to go back.

Most houses were heated with a coal-fired furnace or boiler. A furnace supplied hot air and a boiler supplied a hot water system and/or steam radiators. These systems had to be maintained to provide the right temperature. Coal was delivered in bags on a truck or in a dump truck with a coal chute. The coal chute was inserted through a window that went to a basement coal bin. The chute was metal and made a loud noise when the coal slid down or when the canvas bags were dumped on it. All this was very dirty and dusty and gave the delivery man the look of a coal miner.

Our heating system was steam with steam radiators placed throughout the house. Our furnace needed constant attention: either more coal added or the air door opened for more heat or closed to slow or reduce heat. Often times after supper, I would go play with the fire. I would heat a metal spike red hot and then use it as a wood burning tool to decorate boards or leather. If the furnace or boiler got too hot it would "pop-off" to relieve steam pressure.

The steam system was not as steady as ones in use today.

RAILROAD TRACKS & TRAIN

To get home from the coal yard, we walked on the railroad tracks till we got to the Landham Road bridge. One day while on the tracks we knew the train was due. Roger wanted to see how close to the tracks he could stay while the train went by. The train wasn't going slow. At the last minute Roger backed up. It was scary.

Mom would have thought Roger was like Eddie Haskell in Leave It to Beaver, but she would have been mistaken.

DOING BUSINESS AS A KID

One year for extra money I went through the cold carcass pile of mink and cut out scent glands. I salted them and put them in quart jars that I sent to a trapping supply house. They made mink lure out of them and sold the lure to the trappers.

They forgot to pay me.

Another time during the war when victory gardens were encouraged, I cut a few bundles of beanpoles and took them to a place in Watertown where we often bought a ton or more of ice and where they sold garden supplies. Here again, I never got paid.

Let's put this all down to good learning experiences. Step #1 on the way to becoming a successful businessman: Arrange payment before delivery.

PAYROLL

I was in seventh or eighth grade when I took over payroll duties. I paid bills and signed checks. In agriculture there were no government regulations on withholdings. If a person earned $100, that was the amount of the paycheck.

If I needed money I would write a check for myself. This sounded like a great idea, but by this method Dad knew I would take less than if I were paid an hourly wage. This lasted all through my college days. I always had money, but never thought I could just go and buy a car or spend wildly.

410 SHOTGUN & RATS

My fourth grade hooky partner, Don, had a BB gun. I thought that I should have one also.

"No, you might put someone's eye out, blah blah blah...."

I knew that was true. But did you ever hear of anyone walking around with a black eye patch because he was shot in the eye by a BB gun?

Fast forward to 12 years old. I was the proud owner of a 410 gauge double-barreled Iver Johnson shotgun. It was fun to throw things up in the air and shoot them. And to shoot rats in the feed room. Every day after the mink food was ground and mixed, it was put into nine or 10 large wheelbarrows and taken out to the mink yard. After the feed room was washed and it was quiet, the rats came out. I would sneak back with the 410. If there was a BIG rat I would shoot it. If the rat was smaller, I would wait until two were side by side and kill them both with one shot. The feed room floor was sloped in order to drain the wash water. Once a rat litter was close together and I shot low. The shot bounced off the sloped floor and the litter bodies splattered onto the wall.

Squirrel hunting was fun, but then you had to clean, cook and eat them.

Dad didn't make me eat rats.

OUR DRIVEWAY

Everybody complained about our driveway. Turning from Landham Road, there was a telephone pole right in the middle. You had to pay attention and keep to the right or to the left. Not everyone did. Mom's insurance customers, who parked near the road and entered her office by the front door, often backed into it. Our family was used to avoiding the obstacle so didn't think about it so much, but it was a problem.

One day I wrote a letter to Boston Edison bringing them up to date with our driveway dilemma, then I forgot about it. While waiting for the school bus one morning, a work crew in a large truck showed up and asked where we wanted the pole relocated. I hadn't told anyone about my letter so ran out to the mink yard to explain what was happening to Dad and ran back to get on the bus. That afternoon, getting off the school bus was great. No need to avoid the telephone pole, it had been moved to the side of the driveway.

All you have to do is ask.

DON'T!

I always had trouble with "**DON'T**." Dad would say **DON'T** do this or **DON'T** do that, and up would go a big red flag. I needed a reason. I wanted to know why, or maybe I could do something differently and be O.K.

One morning there was a sick skunk hanging around. It might be rabid or carrying distemper.

Dad said, "Go get the gun and shoot it." That part was O.K. "But after you shoot it, **DON'T** stay around, the fresh scent will get and stay on your clothes."

I should have listened.

I'll admit it now, 70 years later... "Dad, you were right."

We had a few Muscovy ducks. They helped clean up fallen feed under the pens in the mink yard. One duck was sitting on a nest of eggs. They never hatched, and eventually she abandoned them.

Instructions from Dad: "Dig a small hole, put the eggs in, cover them with dirt and **DON'T BREAK THEM!**"

When I broke them, they exploded with such a bad stench I gagged and nearly threw up. Again, who was right, who was wrong?

It was spring, and my job was to clean Ginger the goat's house. All winter her bed of hay had become higher and higher. I loaded the bedding into an old Chevrolet truck with a nine-foot rack body. It took a long time to load. Eventually it would be spread in the field.

"**DON'T** drive out in the field. You will get stuck."

That is where it had to go, so what else could I do?

When Dad got home the truck was parked in the field, stuck. In the next few days I got it out, but I'm sure I heard, "I told you **DON'T**."

PLANE TRIP TO IOWA DURING WWII

Grampa and Gramma Poole paid us a long visit during 1943 and returned home to Diagonal. Gramma had ongoing heart trouble and was not well. Sometime in 1944 Dad decided it would be nice if Nancy and I would visit them.

We were excited about the coming trip, but late in November Gramma died. Dad drove non-stop to get to their home. Arrangements were difficult. Long distance calls were not loud enough or clear enough. On the way out he was in a snowstorm traveling way over the speed limit when he passed an Iowa state trooper. They waved and Dad kept going. When the trooper had seen the Massachusetts license plate, he knew it was an errand of mercy.

Anyhow, Nancy and I thought our trip west was canceled. But that's when it was decided we should go. Grampa would sure love to see us. The trip was planned for Christmas vacation. I remember the trip, and Nancy wrote a detailed 28-page diary.

This account is taken from Nancy's journal and my own memories—we two kids traveled alone halfway across the country during the war.

We two kids left Boston Logan Airport on December 19, 1944. I was 12, Nancy was 14. Logan had one passenger terminal. It was round with all the different airlines around the edge. We flew on a DC-3. We could see houses below. We left at 1:30 p.m. and arrived in New York at 3 p.m. Checked in with United Airlines and were told we had been put off our flight because of priority cargo. While talking with the young woman she got a call, and we were put back on our original Flight 7. She let Chicago know we were coming and told them to try to get us on the Des Moines flight because

"They're two kids traveling alone." Help them all you can. *Note: this was before computers or e-mail.*

During World War II airline travel was strictly regulated. DC-3 aircraft were limited in total carrying weight. Servicemen and women in uniform had top priority over civilians. Priority cargo was critical to the war effort, so sometimes passengers were taken off to meet weight restrictions. However, on shorter flights they would carry a partial load of fuel in order to accommodate more passengers and/or cargo.

Left NYC at 4:10, sunny and snow on the ground. The DC-3 had seven rows of seats, doubles on the left and a single on the right, 21 seats total. Had a very good supper. Landed in Cleveland at 7:10. Left Cleveland at 7:45 with three empty seats. Stewards said empty seats were because the maximum weight had been reached. Arrived in Chicago at 9 p.m.

Miss Thompson helped us check flights to Kansas City by TWA and Braniff, railroad schedules, hotel rooms and all connections. It looked like we would be stuck in Chicago like two lost waifs. Nancy started to wire home, but before she did Miss Thompson came and said connections were so difficult they took off some fuel and let us board the Des Moines flight at the last minute. Arrived in Des Moines, Iowa, at 1 a.m. By now I was tired. While we were in Chicago I could not hear a thing. The planes were not pressurized. My ears stopped up.

Once in Des Moines we went to the railroad station and bought tickets for Diagonal. The train was due to leave at 2:30 a.m. We were able to board the train long before then. I tried to sleep but they kept shuffling the train around and bumping cars. We finally left Des Moines at 4:15 a.m. On the train Nancy met Mary Dowell. Talk about coincidences, Mary lived right across the street from Grampa. We arrived in Diagonal at 7 a.m. Grampa's house was at the opposite edge of the small town. We met Grampa, and I went to bed.

I slept with Grampa in a double bed on a worn out mattress that was shaped like a U. That was O.K., but later I decided that was where Gramma had died. There was no running water. In the kitchen sink was a hand pump for water. At the end of the week I enjoyed a great bath in a galvanized tub in the middle of the kitchen floor. Either my feet were in, and other parts, but not everything at once. The facilities were a two-hole outhouse out back in the COLD. Grampa and I cheated sometimes and used the ash bucket from the coal fire. The ashes were dumped every day.

Diagonal was a typical western town—like in cowboy movies but without the horses. I wasn't used to a town, but it was pretty small. People came to town from the outlying farms to shop for supplies. The main street was wide and the sidewalks were raised wooden ones, so you could load your wagons and buggies easier.

There was a newspaper office, and we were the news. There also was a movie theatre. Diagonal had a community livestock sales barn, a large wooden structure down near the railroad. People sat on wooden benches arranged in a semicircle from ground level up to quite a height. All sorts of livestock, pigs, sheep, lambs, horses and all kinds and ages of cows were bought and sold. It was quite a get together as most everyone knew everyone else.

That Christmas Grampa gave me a horsehair rug or robe, made from a full-size horsehide. I used it on my bed. It was lined with felt and very warm. It was also very heavy to sleep under. I still have it but don't use it.

December 27, we left Diagonal on the train at 5:30 a.m. for Des Moines, changed trains and continued to Waterloo. My mother's older sister, Aunt Maud, met us at the station.

Not much to report about our visit with Uncle Charles and Aunt Maud—we'd had too much visiting. However, Nancy and I both had dental work done by Uncle Charles. Poor Nancy, she had a lot!

Cousin Dick Shane worked in Black's Department store in downtown Waterloo. I rode the bus to meet him and go swimming at the YMCA at noontime—all men and no bathing suits.

We left Waterloo and the big John Deere factory January 5 at 7:15 a.m., crossed the Mississippi River at 9:15, arrived in Chicago at 1:15 p.m., and went by taxi to Uncle Robert's and Aunt Corinne's building. Uncle Robert was one of Mom's older brothers. He was in charge of 15 or 20 elevators in the building. We toured the building and, above all, the elevator machinery. There were four levels below the street. The fourth level had a tunnel that came into the building. This tunnel went all around the city delivering coal and taking out ashes on a small electric train.

On January 9, we called the Palmer House where all the airlines had ticket offices. We were put off our flight for priority reasons. The airline girl (not Miss Thompson) started checking railroads. We were to take the Pacemaker. We had lunch at the Palmer House, paid for by United Air Lines, took a cab to La Salle Street Station, also paid by United Airlines, and got on the train. It was a long night in coach and way late. We had breakfast in the dining car. When we got to New York City, Nancy called Mother. We went from Grand Central Station right to La Guardia Airport and got right on the United flight to Boston with a stop in Providence. Mother and sister Martha met us, and home we went. Martha had a bad burn on her hand from touching a radiator.

Quite a trip! I was glad to be home.

Our new ton-and-a-half truck was awesome.
It had a long wheelbase, a stake body and dual wheels
and was powered with a flathead Ford V-8 engine that
could be revved up and abused and still perform well. This
was the same engine that powered stock car racers that
became so popular in the late '50's. Cars like
Red Cummins's #42 Dynamite Special.

NEW 1945 FORD TRUCK

World War II was over in 1945. There were veterans returning late that year, and all the war-related industries were scaling back. We still took care of Lester Smith's mink ranch and our own mink farm. Dad was still in building mode. Myron Curtis, who had worked through the war at Bath Iron Works in Maine, came to work for us. He helped us build four mink sheds, each 240 feet long.

I was in junior high at Center School in Sudbury Center. I had more time for school things because of more helpers at the mink farm. During the time we took care of Lester Smith's mink, we had used his 1937 Chevrolet truck. It was getting old and tired. In late 1945, Lester was discharged from his Army duty. He got his old truck back.

We bought one of the first available Ford ton-and-a-half stake-body trucks released for civilian use. From 1941 till late 1945 there had been no trucks sold to civilians. Buying this new truck was a milestone event.

On the day we took delivery, Lester's old truck had gone to the Boston fish pier for fish and ice. On the way back it broke down. Our new Ford was sent to the rescue. The load of fish and ice was transferred from the old to the new truck, and the old truck was towed home. Back then you could hook up a chain and do your own towing. Even with the full load and pulling the 1937 Chevy, the new 1945 Ford was peppy.

I would do all sorts of jobs just so I could drive the new truck. This included hauling gravel for our driveway from the gravel pit at Smith's ranch, even though this included loading and unloading by HAND! The new truck's only drawback was that it was not a dump truck.

Deer hunters home from Maine:
Myron Curtis, Dad and a friend

HIGH SCHOOL
fall 1946–spring 1950

CENTER SCHOOL ONCE AGAIN

HUNTING

I had been working all day Saturday. It was probably around pelting time. I was in the bathtub getting shined up for the Saturday night dance at the Town Hall. Dad called upstairs, asking if I wanted to go deer hunting.

That's how he did things, no warning or explanations.

Colebrook, New Hampshire, is north of the 45-degree parallel, close to the Canadian border. O.K., by now it was 7 or 8 o'clock, and we would have to drive all night to get there. We took turns at the wheel. I wasn't old enough for my driver's license, but that didn't seem to matter.

COLEBROOK, N.H.

I don't remember how we obtained our N.H. hunting licenses. When we went to Maine, L. L. Bean was open 24 hours a day and sold hunting licenses. Maybe there was the same sort of place in Concord, N.H. At about 5 a.m. we pulled into Colebrook. The first thing we saw was a telephone pole on fire. After that we found the local small hotel. We were like Mary and Joseph—there was no room at the inn. After all day at work and all night driving, I had to sleep. That meant a big overstuffed chair in the lobby. I had two hours to sleep until sunrise.

Deer hunting meant being out in the woods and on a stand, ready to hunt at sunrise. When hunting with Dad, taking a stand meant just that, you didn't move. I found a "stand" and sat down overlooking a little valley while Dad wandered around in unfamiliar territory. I was all set except for not looking right behind me. Of course that was where I then heard the tiniest little noise.

I turned to see the nicest buck just four or five feet right behind me. Of course by the time I stood up and aimed the rifle, Mr. Buck was long gone. I was just as happy, but then again I wasn't the deer slayer that Dad was. He heard my one ridiculous shot and showed up with an invitation to go to the hotel for lunch. Maybe I would survive after all.

After what was my best lunch ever, we were able to check into the hotel. Dad got settled and announced that he was going back out hunting. I announced that I was going to bed.

I had no problem falling asleep.

EASIER THAN HUNTING

During pelting season in late fall we were busy skinning mink all day, every day, for two to three weeks. After pelting, the only daily tasks were feeding and watering the much smaller breeder herd. That was easier for me than deer hunting.
Dad would go out hunting from early morning until dark with Rene Beland. I would feed and water the mink and have the rest of the day off.

MARTHA'S FOURTH BIRTHDAY

Cousin Herbert from Hawaii came to visit us in Sudbury in May 1948. It was my sister Martha's fourth birthday.

As a hobby, Herb had practiced being a magician so was the guest of honor at Martha's birthday party. It was a super success since all the tricks occurred at close range in the living room instead of on a distant stage.

Herb took odd things out of the guests' ears, cut rope that then wasn't cut, made things disappear and hid coins then got them back—but no live animals.

Perfect for a four-year-old's party.

RED

Myron Curtis, mentioned already, was a carpenter and man-of-many trades of my father's age. An entertaining story-teller from Skowhegan, Maine, he liked working for us with the mink. His son-in-law Red also worked for us.

Red had a problem with alcohol. He had lost his license for DUI and had been in jail. When we were in the mink yard he would shake the gate and pretend he was still in jail and yell, "Let me out! Let me out!" to get a chuckle out of me. I could bug him until he would chase me around the field, and he even threw a hammer at me. I was in ninth grade in high school but too young for a driver's license.

One day Dad and Myron had gone somewhere together and left Red in charge of the farm. I was in school. After school I usually took the second bus home. That bus made a first run to West Sudbury and then back to school for the South Sudbury trip. I had gotten out at 2:30 and was waiting with friends.

A South Sudbury rider came up to me and said, "come on, someone is looking for you."

Then another person found me and said Red was looking for me.

Meanwhile Red was cruising all through the school asking for me. He found Mrs. Bogle and said he was "sorry for all you sons of bitches" stuck at desks.

But he was looking and asking for me.

Finally we met.

"Red, what are you doing here? How did you get here?"

He and his story began to unwind.

At this point the second buses were lined up for loading. But both were behind our beautiful green ton-and-a-half new Ford truck, which was in the Buses Only line.

We had to get out of there. I got Red into the truck, and I got in and drove away.

This was at a small high school in a small town where everybody knew all. To get home I had to go through the center of town then down Concord Road and Route 20 and finally along the home stretch on Landham Road.

When we got home, Myron and Dad listened to my story. Myron told Red to get down cellar to get his final paycheck. Red always liked his jackknife and spent lots of time sharpening it.

I told Myron, "Watch out, he's taking his knife out!"

WHAM! Myron threw a roundhouse right that laid Red flat on the cement floor.

Myron picked up Red's last paycheck and told Red to get in Myron's car for the trip home. Turned out Red had been at Tucker's, a local roadhouse, for long enough to cause all the rumpus.

Next day, Mr. Flynn, our principal, asked me who this Red was. I said I guessed it was someone who used to work for us at the mink farm.

Left to right: Red Joyce, Dad, Martha, Myron and Joey Gallo leaning and sitting on the big new grinder in the driveway the day it was delivered, before it was moved into the feed room and installed

FOOD & WATER, EVERY DAY

Most days on a farm are similar. Every day the mink needed food and water. We needed dependable machinery—a working grinder and mixer in the feed room and a steady water supply—and capable farmhands to see that the mink had fresh food and water, reliable food and water, every day.

FEED ROOM GRINDER & MIXER

Our first grinder was small and underpowered, unable to grind "gill bones" of cod or haddock. The next one, bigger and stronger, was powered by a Model T engine that also powered the mixer with a problematic dual system of flat belts, whose failures of sliding and slipping, among others, were legion. V-belts improved reliability, but power remained a problem.

Tripe from the abattoir needed to be cut into pieces. A scar on my left index finger is where part of my finger joined a piece of tripe, then both went to the grinder to be mink food.

The grinder itself was dangerous.

Then our new 20-horsepower, three-phase electric grinder handled whole tripe and other food without hesitation. It later had a new head shaped to grind frozen and partially thawed 35-pound blocks of fish or meat by-products. We ferried wheelbarrow loads of fish and meat from outside coolers to a table in the feed room that guided the loads to the grinder.

The ground food dropped (via gravity) into a mixer where it was blended with appropriate additives.

THE WATER SYSTEM

Mink need fresh drinking water. Always. Our water supply was crucial.

When the water system at the farm needed upgrading, we bought a new three-horsepower submersible water pump.

I told Dad that I could install the three-phase, 220-volt wiring. The upgrade would be a major improvement. When installed and turned on, it was not.

But as soon as I reversed the wires and turned it on again, it filled a 55-gallon drum in no time at all.

Success was mine, the young electrician!

Cousin Bob Weatherwax and me in Villa Park prior to the
escapade that caused our trip to the Police Station

CHICAGO 1948

It was summer of 1948, and the Weatherwax clan was gath-
ered at Uncle Robert and Aunt Corinne's house In Villa
Park, Illinois. Mom, Nancy, Martha and I drove west in our
1941 Ford car. Dad did not go with us; the mink needed care.
Aunt Maud and Uncle Charles drove east from Iowa. Uncle
Edwin, Aunt Roberta and Cousin Bob came farther east from
California. Cousin Bob was my age.

Aunt Corinne and Uncle Robert worked in downtown
Chicago in the same high-rise building. Cousin Bob and I
went downtown together on the train and were to meet Uncle
Robert and come home with him, again by train. It was just
before the Fourth of July weekend. I never buy fireworks, so
I claim I am innocent, but my mind does fail me once in a
while. The bottom line was that Bob and I had firecrackers
and time on our hands in Chicago. We were in a tall building
that had a central air shaft and elevators with grillwork
doors instead of solid doors. We saw both as perfect targets.

106

Firecrackers tossed into both shafts alerted everyone in the building that it was almost the Fourth of July.

I was still blessed. We weren't caught.

We joined Uncle Robert for the train trip back to his home. As we approached the Villa Park station, Cousin Bob wondered what a handle on a rope hanging down from the ceiling was for. To find out he pulled it. Uncle Robert said it was the fastest stop he had ever seen, maybe an emergency stop. We didn't quite make it all the way into the station.

Our Chicago adventure wasn't over. After dinner, Cousin Bob and I walked down to the station looking for things to blow up. A row of lights looked like fun. We could reach a light and tuck a firecracker next to it. This was awesome, a loud noise... followed by breaking glass... and darkness... followed by a policeman. Next, a ride... Guess where! The Police Station. Remember the old movies with the criminal being grilled under the bright lights?

Remember, this was Villa Park, Illinois.

Question addressed to me: "Where do you live?"

"Sudbury, Massachusetts."

Next question addressed to Bob: "Where do you live?"

"Hollywood, California."

When the police telephoned Uncle Robert's house, Aunt Corinne answered the phone. They said they were the police department and they had two boys who said they were her nephews. She thought it was a joke, laughed and hung up.

By now the cops had us pegged as wise guys. After further explanation and a second phone call to Uncle Robert's house, instead of being sent to the Big House we were rescued by Uncle Robert and Uncle Edwin. They had to act like this was the worst thing that had ever happened.

But I think it brought back their own boyhood escapades.

DRIVER'S LICENSE
July 6, 1948

After our visit in Chicago, Mom, Nancy, Martha and I headed East. I had an appointment at the Massachusetts Department of Motor Vehicles for a driver's license exam. July 4 was over. July 6 was over. I was finally 16.

My life can be divided into two parts. Before having a driver's license, and after having a driver's license. Do not be confused, it had nothing to do with driving or not driving. I had been driving on the road since I was 12 years old. Usually in the Landham Road area or else at night driving Mom.

When you went for a driver's test you needed a vehicle that would pass inspection. Our 1941 Ford car was tired (no pun intended) by 1948, and it had just been all the way to Chicago and back. It didn't have a good emergency brake. So it was decided that I would take the driver's exam in the 1945 truck. With its long wheel base it couldn't turn as sharply as a car. It wouldn't do a three-point turn or parallel park. You had to double clutch in order not to grind the gears.

I passed the driver's test. I was free, free at last.

My first assignment was, "Go to the hardware store."

I had second thoughts that didn't last long.

DRIVING FOR AUBREY BORDEN

Aubrey Borden was a local dairy farmer and one of three Sudbury Selectmen. I was friendly with his son Jackie, who was younger than I. Aubrey owned a Ford dump truck that he rented out to the State. His hired hand Benny would help milking the cows in the morning and then take the truck out for State work.

Once in a while on a snowy or icy evening I might be called to drive his truck on Route 20. It was a blast—from the Sudbury sandpit east to the Watertown town line or west to the Marlborough line. I could go through the Weston lights without stopping.

You had to keep moving to spread sand.

COW MANURE & SHAVINGS

Another Aubrey job was delivering loads of cow manure. Nothing was too good for the fancy gardens and immaculate lawns in the Newton-Wellesley area. When Jackie and I arrived at our destination, we would have to find out exactly where to dump the load. Often the garden was away from the road or driveway, and most people had no idea—until it was too late—how backing over the lawn would destroy it and what a mess the cow manure would make.

Sometimes I had to get up early and drive to a saw mill in Derry, New Hampshire, to get a load of wood shavings used for cow bedding. That was cool, and of course I never got to school on time after a N.H. run.

Delivering a load of sweet corn to the Boston produce market was always good for some kind of excitement, such as inadvertently dumping empty returnable bushel boxes on the road at the traffic circle or driving up onto the sidewalk in Waltham to avoid an accident.

THE MINK YARD
Two wooden mink houses, back left, had been moved
from across the street in 1939. The outside pens in
the foreground were soon torn down. Four newer
mink sheds, back right, were permanent and 100-foot
extensions were added to each of them.

ADDING MINK PENS

One morning in the summer Dad said, "Take the truck to Framingham Lumber."

That was the way he was. There was no easing into things that needed to be done. I was to pick up a load of eight-foot cedar posts that were six inches in diameter. There were now four mink sheds 240 feet long, and we were going to add 100 feet in length to each one.

Buying the posts was the easy part. But each of the 130 three-foot holes had to be dug by hand! *This was before there were tractor-powered post-hole diggers.* Then the posts were dropped in, lined up and tamped down, adding room for more than 300 breeder pens and 600 pelting pens.

A Big Job!

110

BEDDING MINK

I remember once when I was in fourth grade Dad was busy so I had to stay home from school in a heavy spring rainstorm to bed the mink.

I loaded a wheelbarrow with hay and headed for an outside row of breeding pens. Wearing a heavy glove on my left hand, I carefully opened each nest box, pushing the mink out of the box and into the pen. Holding the mink in the pen with my gloved hand blocking the opening between box and pen, I cleaned out the box with a scraper in my right hand, put clean hay in and quickly shut the nest box. All without letting a mink loose.

The outside pens did not have a fence, so an escaped mink would have been difficult or impossible to catch. There was a mink-proof fence around the four newer sheds so escaped mink were catchable.

CLEANING UP

Once a week, usually a Saturday, was clean-up day.

Manure: We raked it from under the pens into piles in the aisles, scooped it into a wheelbarrow, pushed the wheelbarrow up a wooden ramp and dumped the manure on the truck. Next stop was Bordens' corn field, where we shoveled it all out. It was a big job that took most of the day.

Sometimes people complained of the odor, but often that was only when the clean-up disturbed things.

111

BOSTON FISH PIER

Before I had my driver's license, other drivers had done the trucking needed to buy fish and slaughterhouse byproducts— protein ingredients of mink food. For several years when the herd was small, we bought filleted cod or haddock leftovers at the fish pier in Boston.

Now I was the truck driver! I would put 12 or 15 empty barrels—these were 55-gallon drums—in the new truck and head for Boston on Route 20. It took about an hour, going through Wayland, Weston, and Watertown to Atlantic Avenue in Boston and the fish pier on Northern Avenue. Atlantic Avenue was brutal: no overhead section, but countless trucks and cars and taxis, honking horns, and a freight train making local deliveries right down the middle of the street. Taxis tried to edge me out but the truck body stuck out, and when it was over a taxi fender, guess who won!

This was the North End where the Great Molasses Flood occurred in 1919. I could still smell the results.

I would arrive mid-morning in order to arrange with a fish-cutting outfit to buy several barrels of gurry, the waste parts after filleting fish. Fishing boats offloaded their catches into old-fashioned dump carts that were pulled by Ford tractors to the cutting house. Each cutting house might have a crew of 10 filleting haddock and tossing leftovers into a barrel. I would roll their barrel out to the truck, then pitch the fish from street level to a drum on the truck and return their barrel. Then do it all again, and again, and again...

It took most of the day. No wonder I wanted a truck with a hydraulic tailgate!

I headed home in afternoon traffic, stopping in Watertown to buy a ton of ice. When I got back to the farm, I unloaded ice and the fish gurry in layers into the cooler—that would last for about a week.

BRIGHTON ABATTOIR

The Brighton Cattle Market was first established in 1776 on a site in Brighton, Massachusetts, to supply meat to General Washington's Army. By the middle of the 19th century a stockyard next to the train tracks held cattle ready to be processed at the abattoir and rendering house.

With that history behind me, I went to Brighten to buy tripe, beef spleens, lungs, milk bags and liver. Early on I had to learn how to buy correctly for the needs of the mink farm.

BRAINS

On one of my trips home from the Brighton slaughterhouses I had only a few boxes of calf brains and a 300-pound bar of ice. It was such a tiny load that I did not tie it on. The ice against the headboard would melt and hold itself on, and the box would hold them both on—or so I thought.

On Route 20 at Watertown Square I stopped at a red light. When the light turned green, I forgot that I needed a careful start. That traffic circle had probably seen its share of various incidents over the years, but maybe not such a gooey mess.

I stopped to retrieve it, but nobody else did. There was no way to clean up the spilled brains Some boxes were O.K., and I salvaged some ice. Then I kept going.

Lesson learned: Use my brain, and always tie up the load.

TIVERTON FISH

In July 1948 a major problem was food supply. Our herd was growing. With four covered sheds each being lengthened to total 340 feet for many more mink, we needed large quantities of fish and meat. Other mink farmers went to the Boston fish pier, which we had done for years. But now it was difficult to get a steady supply that we could count on.

Instead, in the spring of the year Poole Mink Farm had bought 100,000 pounds of sea robins from a fish run caught off the coast of Rhode Island. Sea robins were tasty but too bony for human consumption—perfect for mink. These fish were frozen in 40-pound blocks and stored in a large warehouse freezer in Tiverton, Rhode Island. I hauled three or four tons of frozen fish each week.

My first trip was in a rainstorm. After dark in July was cooler, but it was still hot. So we carried old rugs and canvas to line the truck sides and cover the load of frozen fish. Dad rode shotgun and showed me the way. In Millis, Massachusetts, the road turned more than 90 degrees and the truck started to spin out—**the road was wet!** I recovered the spin. Dad commented that he knew the bad curve was there, but he wanted ME to remember it. I still do!

On later trips I drove the truck to school so as to get an earlier start. The 60-mile one-way trip, mostly on old back roads, took more than two hours. I enjoyed shifting down on the hills and through the towns.

A worker rolled out pallets of frozen fish. We piled the blocks tight on the truck and covered them. The blocks stayed frozen until packed away in the storage cooler at home. Each day the top layer would thaw enough to go through the grinder. On the way home I often stopped at the diner in Rumford, Rhode Island, for steak, potatoes, green beans, a glass of milk and a piece of pie, all for about $1.

PEMBROKE COLLEGE FRIENDS

Nancy was a sophomore at Pembroke College in Providence, Rhode Island. Pembroke was a women's college affiliated with Brown University, both located on a hill overlooking downtown Providence. The young women could take classes from the Brown professors.

Once in a while I would detour there and pick up her or one of her college friends and continue to the freezer in Tiverton. Those girls didn't know anything about trucks or trucking, and I didn't know anything about college girls or older women, so it was a fun time for all.

On the fish truck with me the girls got to see some of the real world. It was a great escape or diversion from classes, books and homework. My favorite was Priscilla Talcott. She came home with Nancy once in a while. She even rode with me on my motorcycle. I fell in love with Priscilla!

On the way home from Tiverton, driving through Providence to drop off any passenger(s) was challenging. Steep hills with an overloaded truck of frozen fish required first gear and hopes that you didn't need to stop and restart often.

DAD & CAVICCHIOS' TRACTOR

Manure disposal was a big job to keep up with. All the pens were about two feet off the ground. Manure was raked into the aisle, then scooped into a wheelbarrow and either spread on the field or wheeled up a ramp and dumped on the truck. Once spread out in the field, it was harrowed into the soil to cut down on the smell. We borrowed Cavicchios' tractor for this job. I was harrowing, which meant going across the field, lifting the harrow just before the ditch and then turning around by using the brake on one back wheel or the other. The steering wheel didn't work because the weight of the harrow lifted most of the weight on the front end. Dad came by and asked me to go to Brighton for some meat at the slaughterhouses.

When I got back I asked where the tractor was. It was at Bill Brown's Auto Body Shop for repairs to the front and hood. It hadn't turned the way he expected and the way he saw me do it.

He had driven it into the ditch.

A SEEING-EYE DAUGHTER

Mr. Cavicchio lived about a mile from his farm. Over time he became increasingly blind. He had two children who often went with him to work in his greenhouse. On the way home Celia, his daughter, acted as his seeing-eye dog while he drove the car.

"A little more this way" or "Back that way" helped keep him going in the right direction.

The ultimate direction was, "WAVE, it's the Chief of Police!"

DAD & BERT SNOW'S DUMP TRUCK

Bert Snow was a local character. After the war ended he bought an Allis Chalmers shovel dozer. He also had a small dozer and a large FORD dump truck. He mostly worked preparing house sites in Weston, Massachusetts, but helped us during the breeding season in March, when he couldn't do earthwork. Once in a while I delivered loam for Bert.

Dad planned to borrow Bert Snow's truck to take a load of gravel home. I tried to explain the two-speed rear axle. Anyway, he got the gravel and got home just fine.

But he failed to release the tailgate when he went to dump the load. All the weight of the gravel went to the back and, instead of dumping, the front of the truck went up in the air. Now with the pressure on the tailgate it was impossible to release the tailgate. The truck cab and front end wouldn't come down until he shoveled off some of the load by hand.

MY "CLASS A" TRUCK LICENSE

At that time our State Motor Vehicle Department, in their wisdom to create more regulations, decided to change drivers' licenses to A, B and C. Class A was for all vehicles, including tractor trailers. Class B was small trucks, and Class C was automobiles. Bert urged me to put in for Class A, which at the beginning was issued under a grandfather clause, in other words, for anyone who already drove some sort of truck and trailer. I never had to take a Class A test. But much later, when renting a tractor trailer, I did have to pass a test for a Ryder rental tractor and semi-trailer.

117

WESTON WRECKER

One winter day when it had started to snow I was sent to Brighton for meat. With just the breeder herd to feed we didn't need much meat, thus I was driving the '41 Ford *(photo opposite page)*. On the way home coming into Weston I looked where I was steering and that was different than where I was going. There were three-week-old icy snow banks from a previous snowstorm. I was headed directly to the one on the right side of the road.

I made my all-time best stop—from 35 mph to zero in the length of the car. It stalled, but when I re-started it the engine made a terrible noise and I had to shut it down immediately. I thought it was a major fault. I opened up the hood and found a wooden grate marker hitting the fan. Removing that solved the bad noise, but I was on top of the plowed snow bank with no traction. I called a nearby wrecker and with difficulty was back on all four wheels. The set of tire chains on the wrecker had thrown all sorts of snow on top of the car. I only had about $4 with me, but that was O.K.

No one at home ever knew.

*Sometimes it would be a big job to dig out
and take care of all the farm chores.*

WINTER PARKING

Another snowy day I drove the car into the driveway. It was slippery, and I was lazy. I knew that I could just spin to turn around, instead of pulling in and backing up. You need a little speed to spin, which I had. But instead of the back spinning, the front slipped and the car hit the front of the still-rather-new parked truck and bounced back. Today it would be a reportable offense, two vehicles involved.

I parked the car in the usual place, got out and prepared to check out the damage. No dents on the car fender. I checked the truck, no dents. Just a little truck green paint on the car. And nobody looking out the window! How so? The truck was parked with the front wheels turned toward the car. The car bumper hit the truck tire and bounced me back.

I really was blessed. All my spinning and sliding practices could be saved for later use at college.

119

DENNY WHITWORTH

Denny Whitworth, a good friend, was a year behind me in school. He drove a Model A Ford. Oftentimes we would meet before school and follow each other there. We got in the habit of passing each other on the wrong side on Landham Road. I would be way over on the left side, and Denny would be way over on his left side.

All was O.K. until one morning when I saw the Model A coming toward me. I pulled over to the left to do our usual wrong-side pass, and the Model A pulled over not to my right, as expected, but farther to my left. Guess what, it was Denny's father, Jack! We did not crash head-on, but that was the end of the high jinx.

LATIN SCHOLAR

One high school day still stands out vividly in my mind. I was between classes, minding my own business, walking down the hall with my hands in my pockerts and my thumbs out, and behold, who should stop me but Mr. Crowley, my Latin teacher. He had a sad look on his face and both good and bad news according to which side you were on. For me it was great news. My marks in Latin I were so bad I would not be allowed to take Latin II.

This changed my whole future. When applying for college I didn't have a second language, but I was able to work around that. I didn't need SAT's. That is another useless addition of modern life.

ANOTHER HURRICANE

One time I left for Tiverton early in the morning. I didn't realize that I was driving into a hurricane. No radio in the truck, and none of the weather warnings that we get nowadays. Crossing over the Mount Hope Bridge on the way down, the empty truck was blown to the side. I knew it was windy but didn't know it was the beginning of a hurricane.

I pulled into the loading dock of a large cold-storage warehouse next to a tidal river in Tiverton to load up with frozen fish. Weather got worse.

Before I got a full load Mike said I should cover what I had and, "GET OUT OF HERE!"

Twenty minutes later, where the truck had been parked was under six to eight feet of water.

On the way home with a partial load, the traffic came to a stop. I stayed through the worst of the storm with six other people in a stopped Greyhound bus. At first we could look down the street. Afterward, there were so many downed branches we could barely see the road.

I got going again and came to a place with water over the road. The truck cab was high, and because of the frozen fish I thought I'd better keep going. The water level was deeper than I hoped for. It rose above the floor of the cab three or four inches. Because the distributor is low on the end near the crank shaft, it got wet and the motor stalled. A National Guard truck (duck) came along and stopped, pulled me out and kept going until my truck restarted.

I was still blessed. I got home that afternoon. Everyone was really relieved to see the truck, the load of fish and me, in that order.

PIPELINE

Sometime before 1949 a natural gas pipeline was planned to extend from Texas to the Boston area. It cut across a corner of our land. To me this meant excitement. The first hint that it was actually to be built was surveyors coming through.

Some people didn't want it because it might blow up. It might be dangerous. But on it came.

The next crew came with chainsaws, cutting down about a 40-foot-wide right of way. Those men were tough. They worked from 6 a.m. until 6 p.m., running chainsaws that were much heavier than the chainsaws of today.

As an aside, I must admit to a longtime addiction. No, not alcohol or tobacco. Yes, starting and running heavy equipment, like backhoes and bulldozers. This was before there were machines like excavators and the use of high-pressure hydraulics.

Back to the pipeline. If it was easy going, a large ditch digger dug a deep ditch using a huge rotary wheel with buckets all around. If it was tough digging, a backhoe run by cables took over—no hydraulics. Two tractor-trailers then hauled long lengths of two- or three-foot diameter pipe that were laid out along the ditch. Welders connected the sections of pipe. Workers coated the pipeline with tar, and then wrapped some sort of covering around the pipe.

Beyond our house was a swampy meadow and then the brook. One of the work trucks was a brand new Ford truck tractor. It had 700 total miles and already was a mess. When the truck hauling the pipe got stuck, pretty often, they hooked up the cable winch on a Caterpillar D-4 and dragged the truck through the swamp. All the hummocks were forced right up under the hood into the truck engine compartment.

What a mess.

I was able to start the Unit cable backhoe one night but not able to control the cable. I might mess up equipment, but I wouldn't break or destroy anything. The following morning workers had to pull the cable out and then re-roll it onto the cable drums. The next night there was a guard near the parked machinery.

Crossing the brook was the next obstacle. An International TD-24, the largest bulldozer made at that time, worked all day creating a giant stockpile of loam, ready to dam the brook the following day so that the pipe could be laid across.

That evening I got the TD-24 started—what a feeling of power! Jackie was with me. I started up the stockpile. It was so steep that all you could see was the sky. I got to the top and the dozer started dipping dramatically down the other side, with Jackie yelling, "stop, Stop, STOP!" That was fun.

Another day we were in Denny's Jeep going to another site to watch the pipeline activity. The track was so steep we couldn't get the four-wheel-drive Jeep up the hill. Then along came the foreman in a '47 Chevrolet car, and he drove right up the hill. He knew what he was doing.

After all the work by big machinery digging and assembling, smaller side-boom Cat D-7's and D-8's placed the finished pipe in the trench. One little Cat with a side boom and cable blade did most of the backfilling of the trench.

Overseeing the pipeline—and illicitly operating machines at night—kept Denny and me busy all summer.

SAD ADVENTURES WITH THE BORDENS' PICKUP TRUCK

The Bordens had a small 1937 International pickup truck. It was old fashioned: the cab was framed with wood covered with metal panels. One Sunday afternoon, Jackie, Denny and I were trying to find something to do. Denny was Jackie's neighbor. We decided to take a ride up Old County Road with the pickup truck. The paving soon turned to gravel. Never any traffic.

I was driving, and it was fun to skid back and forth. That is a good exercise to learn to handle a truck or any vehicle. The next thing I knew, we were skidding more than we wanted to and, as we were broadside to the road, the back corner of the truck body clipped a tree. When we looked back, the body was just barely balancing on the back. Then it fell off and rolled into the street. We looked back and thought that was the funniest thing we had ever seen. We backed up and put the body back on, but failed to re-secure it with bolts.

Fast forward to Monday. Jackie's father, Aubrey, often took five or six milk jugs to Twin Maple Dairy in Saxonville. He backed up to the milk-house on the edge of the lawn to load the jugs. One jug at a time he placed on the back of the truck and then slid forward to the front. The same for the rest. When he got to the dairy, he got on the truck and moved them all to the back, ready for unloading. As he stepped off, the loose body tipped up. Talk about spilled milk, this was it! As we left school that afternoon, we saw Jackie's dad discussing something with Jackie. I knew enough to stay away.

Two weeks later on Sunday afternoon, it was the same scene: Jackie, Denny and me. The difference was Jackie was driving. I was in the middle. Denny was on my other side.

Same skidding back and forth, same place going down hill on the gravel, but this time with entirely different results. The truck came around sideways, I looked out the side window and instead of looking off to the horizon, I was looking straight down to the road. When the side of the truck hit the road, the roof of the cab opened up where it joined the back of the cab, and I went flying out ahead of the truck. I bounced a couple of times on the road, and then saw the truck rolling over on top of me. I was pinned down between the body and the wishbone.

Next was silence.

Jackie saw Denny. "Are you O.K.?"

"Yes. Are you O.K.?"

"Yes. Where's Jim?"

"I'm O.K., I'm down here. Get me out."

The truck landed on its side, a back tire flat on the road. They rolled the truck off me, and I was free. Once the battery was put back, we started the truck and drove home.

Every piece of metal was wrinkled, and all of the glass smashed and gone. Aubrey Borden parked the wreck in front of his barn for the whole world to see. I was bumps and bruises, from gritting my teeth and hitting the road. I had to see a dentist. I was wearing a WWII leather bomber jacket. It was all cut up, mostly in the back.

In school the next day, Ann Burns was sad. She liked to wear the coat once in a while. The jacket saved me a lot of cuts. Jackie and I found out the problem. When coasting down the hill, the truck came out of gear. And when it was coasting in neutral there was no way to throttle it and straighten out.

This time I was alive and really blessed.

Pre-Broadway stars: Marcia Gaughan as Julie Harris and me as Elmer Tuttle in "June Mad," a comedy in three acts...

126

"JUNE MAD" &
"EVER SINCE EVE"

Sudbury High School always put on an annual senior play in December. Lack of actors meant both juniors and seniors were in the plays. I had never thought about it and had no ambition to be an actor.

When I was a junior and "June Mad" practice got closer, the need for more actors and actresses became apparent. Not only that, but pressure to join the cast increased. Play practice was held in the evening upstairs in the Town Hall, and it was fun to go out in the evening, so the other actors talked me into it.

I agreed to act, but was not destined for stardom. No Emmy awards. I had a kissing part and Mrs. Bogle, one of the teachers, wanted to help me be more realistic.

Often times I drove the truck to practice because the car was being used. This came in handy for collecting furniture that was needed for props.

Mrs. Alexander was helping, and when a large upholstered chair was needed, two of us went in the truck to fetch the chair from her house. We didn't knock. We entered and saw her husband, Algy, sitting in his favorite chair, reading. Without a word we picked up the chair Algy was not sitting in and walked out. You would have had to have known Algy to get the full effect of our visit—it was better than our parts in the play!

So my acting career first included "June Mad" then "Ever Since Eve" the following year. *I saved both play books but have not a clue as to what they were about.*

EASTERN STATES EXPOSITION

Mr. Flynn, the principal at the Sudbury Center School, was gassed in France in World War I. When he spoke to us he always had to clear his throat. One time he told us if we ever had a chance to go to the Eastern States Exposition in Springfield, Massachusetts we should go. We wouldn't be skipping school, and we would be learning much more than the same day at school.

Autumn arrived and also fair season. Mom and a friend of hers and Denny and I went to the fair. The fairground had six permanent buildings. One for each New England state—each year a new exhibit. It took all day to cover the fairgrounds. The sights and smells and memories have lasted a lifetime.

Farmers brought all sorts of animals and stayed in a campground or near their animals for the week of the fair. Horse and oxen pulls, judging of all sorts, animals, vegetables, poultry, foods and crafts. Barns were full of animals: one for horses, one for cows, another for sheep, another for goats, another for pigs and another for ducks and chickens. Dogs showed off their herding skills. It all went on and on.

Nothing smelled quite like fair food: fried peppers, fried onions, hot dogs and sausages. Many churches provided specialty meals for the hungry crowds.

People left because they were exhausted, not because they had seen it all.

Mr. Flynn was right. It was a sight to behold and remember.

SELLING MAGAZINES

Sudbury High School didn't have a gymnasium. The only sport we had was baseball. Once in a while there would be a high school meeting to discuss supporting the baseball team. The only thing needed was uniforms and equipment for the team. The money-making scheme was to sell magazine subscriptions. We seniors tried and failed. We didn't sell a single subscription. At the next sports meeting it was made very clear that the seniors were not co-operating. Our class was so small that we could discuss and decide a course of action needed. Our class president (me) steered us to go out the next day and sell magazines instead of attending school. That was a bad decision.

The next day all 14 magazine salespersons scoured the town. By 10 or 11 a.m. we needed to rethink our plan. By then we knew we were in trouble, so we thought we might as well make the most of it. We would all just skip school and go to Boston for the rest of the day. I had more support than on previous hooky days. We went to a stage show and saw Art Mooney and his Four Leaf Clover Band. The movie was "The Outlaw," starring Jane Russell. WOW! Jane Russell appeared live in the stage show. The next day in school it was difficult trying to explain that we had tried to sell magazines, and failed, so then went to Boston.

We did not sell a single magazine subscription.

FIRES

Right next to the school was a siren that blew every noontime. It could be heard all over town. It also blew to announce fires so the volunteer fireman would respond. We were not supposed to leave the school grounds, but if the juniors or seniors were outside when the whistle blew, we were off.

If it was a fire in the woods we would show up, grab an Indian pump from the fire truck and help out. An Indian pump was worn like a backpack, filled with water, with a lever to create water pressure and a small hose and nozzle to spray the fire. The problem for all of us came later on at home when our nice school clothes, especially our shoes, were noticed.

The fire station was located in the basement of the Town Hall. Mr. Quinn was the janitor of the Town Hall and lived right next door. His responsibility was to drive the fire truck to the fire. The fire truck was a 1940's Ford. It was like the mink farm truck and was difficult to shift, needing to be double-clutched. Mr. Quinn ground all the gears.

Oh how I wanted to drive that fire truck. Then the gears wouldn't grind!

TRIP TO WASHINGTON, D.C.

Our senior class trip was to Washington, D.C. There were 14 members of the class of 1950. Six boys and eight girls. I don't remember how we financed our trip. We were two carloads full. Thirteen class members and two chaperons. Mrs. Bogle, our homeroom teacher, chaperoned the girls and Mr. Hawes chaperoned the boys. The cars large enough to carry us were called beach wagons.

We drove from Sudbury to Gettysburg, Pennsylvania. Next day we saw the battlefield and other interesting sites. Then a shorter drive took us to Washington. Mr. Hawes made sure we got to see the usual sights, such as the Supreme Court, the House of Representatives, the Senate and the FBI building— all non-stop. Homeward bound included an overnight stop in New York City. That stop is a blur in my mind.

We all felt bad that Bob Johnson wasn't able to go on the trip with us. His mother had been a teacher years before. She was even a substitute once in a while for our class. Every year in the spring Bob would have the worst case of spring fever of anyone in the whole school. Our Washington trip was in the spring and, as usual, Bob had completely shut down to the point he needed good or better marks in order to graduate. Thus no trip for him.

But everyone in our class did graduate.

GRADUATION

I think I should have graduated from Mrs. Johnson's first and second grades. They were much harder than all the rest leading up to twelfth grade, senior year, at Sudbury High in 1950.

We were prepared in those early grades: reading and writing and arithmetic and the Palmer method of cursive writing with stick figures and O's. Reading included phonics. We had plays, they were popular. Mrs. J. played music on the piano. We sang songs that were understood by both classes and were usually fun.

We got the basics.

My favorite first grade song:

> *Who carries off our rubbers*
> *and hides them in the snow,*
> *So that we cannot find them*
> *when we to school must go?*
> *It's Jimmy, our puppy,*
> *an imp and full of fun,*
> *It's Jimmy, our puppy,*
> *who's always on the run!"*

I remember the tune!

THE CLASS PRESIDENT'S WELCOME ADDRESS

Now we were finally ready for our own graduation from high school. As class president I was in charge of the welcome address. It didn't cause any teary eyes:

Ladies and Gentlemen, Parents and Friends:
We, the class of 1950, come before you this evening to try and show you what progress we have made during our high school career. The last four years have been busy ones, and each year has seen its own accomplishments.

Tonight we realize that our high school days are over and as we think back at the experiences met together, we wish to thank everyone who has helped make these times possible. We all appreciate the many fine things our teachers have done for us and the things fellow students have done to make our stay at Sudbury High a useful and memorable one.

We welcome all you friends who have shown your interest by coming tonight and hope you will long remember, with a thrill of pleasure, the association of this hour.

I still have a copy so that it may be filed with Abraham Lincoln's Gettysburg address.

THE GRAND MARCH

A grand march usually happened once at each formal dance. Fellows would choose partners and line up as couples to march around the hall, as directed, splitting up for the second round—boys to the left and girls to the right, coming back together to alternate direction as couples—called a grand right and left, and other special moves.

I led the march at our junior prom and again at our senior reception when I was class president.

SENIOR RECEPTION

For the senior reception I had a date with Mary Elizabeth Gafney, a sophomore.

I must apologize to Marcia. She and I had gone to all the same classes all 12 years until I missed Latin II. We had gone to corn husking parties and barn parties. I should have asked her to the senior reception.

CLASSMATES

The Lloyd twins were in school with us just during the war. *John died in Lancaster (I think), Massachusetts, in the late 1990's. A year after John's died, Richard visited the grave site and was found dead on John's grave.*

After eighth grade Roger MacArthur and his siblings moved from Sudbury to Southborough, Massachusetts, about 10 miles away, to live with their mother and father. *On July 31, 1973, Roger was on Delta flight #723 from Manchester, New Hampshire, that crashed in the fog short of the runway at Logan Airport in Boston, killing a total of 90 passengers and crew.*

SENIOR THOUGHTS

It was a great time to be school kids. We had been old fashioned, and now there were new ways of doing things. The war years were over. We must not forget the sacrifices made by those just before us.

I think graduation meant more to parents and friends than to us. At least I felt that way. I hope our teachers were proud of us.

Another love: AIRPLANES!
I took flying lessons whenever I could afford them.
I piloted an Aeronca Champ with a 65-horsepower
engine and later with an 85-horsepower engine. Photo
above probably taken at the airport in Marborough,
Massachusetts. When in college, I took more lessons at the
airport in Burlington, Vermont.

A VERY BUSY YEAR
summer 1950–summer 1951

SUMMER, MORE MINK

The summer after graduation was my time of reflection. I always knew I was expected to journey on to college. Dad made sure of that.

Meanwhile day-to-day life on the mink farm was the reality. We wheeled 10 large wheelbarrows of food out to various sections of the mink yard every day. It took three people all afternoon just to feed the mink. Each of us put food in a 12-quart bucket and held it on our left hip with our right hand scooping feed, one pen at a time, for 5,000 pens. As we went down one side of each section, we placed a handful, more or less, on every wire cage—then continued feeding back up the other side, down the next section and back, down and back, down and back, down and back… quickly walking more than a mile. A dirty, heavy and tiresome job.

Plus, Dad always reminded us to return empty wheelbarrows to the feed room ready for the next day. An extra trip to return a wheelbarrow was not tolerated.

COLLEGE, A LONG WAY ROUND

I never took any SAT's. I still don't know what SAT stands for. I liked the sound of a college in Ohio. It had a work-study program. Another school sounded possible: Embry-Riddle School of Aviation in Opa-Locka, Florida, near Miami. They had a course in Design Engineering and Maintenance.

With three speeding tickets, it was time to "Get out of Dodge." Mom and Dad drove me to Logan Airport. I entered the terminal. There was American Airlines to Ohio, and right at the next counter was Eastern Airlines to Florida.

The choice was mine.

Swaying palm trees and warm ocean breezes won.

AVIATION SCHOOL, BRIEFLY

Upon arrival, Embry-Riddle did not look at all like its brochure. During World War II there were three major airports in Miami, all in a row. Embry-Riddle was the farthest north, right on the edge of the Okefenokee Swamp with a large airplane hanger, leftovers from an old Navy base and old run-down barracks. They did have a swimming pool, as advertised, but it was half full with scummy stagnant water.

I started out with all engineering classes. I wanted to be fixing airplanes. Flying lessons and pilot training were also offered. That would have been great, but I didn't think I could afford flying lessons. I was getting good marks in my classes, but I was not busy enough. I thought I could find a job and also keep up with the studies. Dad backed me up with money to buy a Cushman motor scooter. I hit the road looking for a job with no positive results. I knew if I wrote home I would get a "stick it out a bit longer" answer.

Add in some homesickness and I decided, "Sudbury, here I come."

HOME FROM FLORIDA

I knew Dad would not turn down my November mink pelting skills, so I packed my footlocker, tied it on my scooter, took it to the station and sent it home via Railway Express. My next move was a letter home; then I left before I could get a reply.

The first day was all day at 30 or 35 miles per hour, and I was still in Florida. Overnights were mostly at "Tourist Homes." Motels did not exist. Every day I would send a postcard home. U.S. Route 1 all the way, eight full days. The only trouble was a squeak in the front end. Stopped at gas stations for my usual gallon of gas and a squirt of grease.

Many years later, I was enjoying a visit to the Smithsonian Institute. I was in the transportation section and there for the whole world to see was my bright red Cushman motor scooter with the little peddle foot kick starter.

The scooter ride was similar to riding a horse: a slow ride out in all kinds of weather and everything to see. Life in the slow lane. Traveling through New York City was a little daunting—too much traffic, too many tractor trailers, buses and cars.

I was entering the home stretch. I suppose home folks were as happy to see me as I was to see them, but not so happy that I had quit school.

One thing I should have done was to keep notes on that trip to update my memory.

WHAT NEXT?
DEAN ACADEMY

It was the middle of December 1950. I had no plans for my future. Not so with Dad. He came out with one of his life-changing commands: I had an appointment to meet President Garner at Dean Academy and Junior College, 20 miles away in Franklin, Massachusetts. Dean Academy had a good sports record and was slowly evolving into what is now Dean College.

On my way to Franklin I had a flat tire, so I arrived late for the appointment with dirty hands. So much for first impressions. We (the president and I) decided I would take physics, chemistry, algebra and geometry. If I started right away, mid-December, I could take all the first semester finals held in mid-January. These were courses I had already taken at Sudbury High School. But I would have a stronger record to apply to college if I was a Dean Academy graduate. If I passed the first semester final exams I would get full credit for the semester. If I didn't pass the exams it wouldn't be held against me.

It was a win-win situation, and I passed all four.

A DAY STUDENT

To start out I was a day student and drove 40 miles round trip. Dad's thought was that I would live in the dorm the second semester. But the commuting worked out so well that I remained a day student. Dad liked my help on the farm at the end of the day. Besides, I hadn't looked forward to being the only new student in the dorm.

In a small town everyone seems to know what people do. In my case I was able to give a neighbor a ride from Sudbury to her job in Framingham as I passed through. Homeward bound on Friday afternoons, I was available to provide rides from Franklin to the train station in Framingham, handy for kids going home to Connecticut for the weekend. I once gave a ride to Lynn Faith, daughter of bandleader Percy Faith.

MINK FARM ROOTS

One day I was in the Dean library and was reminded of my mink farm roots.

My coat was on the back of my chair. A dog came in and I sensed trouble. My leather coat had mink smells undetectable to people, but not dogs. The dog was making the rounds of students reading or studying. When he got to me he was intrigued by an unfamiliar odor. By this time the dog was the center of attraction. In fact, he was so attracted that he thought he would be pleased to add to the smell and started to lift his leg. I pretended to pat him but gave him a little chop above his nose. That seemed to do the trick. With everyone watching he moved on to explore other smells and left me a nice dry sweet-smelling coat.

141

SUMMER 1951

During the summer of 1951, I was home and had use of the car when it was available. The red Cushman motor scooter had done it's duty but didn't want to go to college. Money, or lack thereof, didn't permit me to buy a car.

A motorcycle was the solution. I didn't belong nor did I want to belong to a biker group. It was a question of transportation. The scooter went "off to the Smithsonian."

I found two Harleys: one was a 1937 model 74, the other was a 1939 model 74 basket case. A Harley was manufactured by the Harley-Davidson Company. The model 74 was an engine with 74-cubic-inches displacement—BIG for that time—a hand shift and a foot clutch. The 1939 basket case was completely disassembled with all the parts in a basket. My next step was to decide which 1939 parts were better than the 1937 and install them. My friend Larry Evans was a great help.

Dad was worried about the combination of me and my motorcycle. He soon found out that I was careful, and things were O.K. Even Police Chief McGovern borrowed it to ride in the Fourth of July parade.

I liked to retard the sparks when coming home late at night so it would produce a series of backfires as I slowed down. One night I came up over a hill and directly in front were two skunks. If I hit one it might have caused a spill, to say nothing of how I might smell. I lifted my legs and went right between them.

I was still blessed.

NOT EXTRAVAGANT

My motorcycle used 90-weight oil for two reasons: it was air cooled and did not have an oil filter. Being air cooled, it ran hotter so needed a thicker oil. With no oil filter, little by little it dripped oil on the final drive chain. Most gas stations didn't carry 90 oil, so to avoid hassle I ordered a case.

Dad thought I was being extravagant and let me know this very directly, up one side and down the other.

Soon it was my turn. I was up in the loft of the garage that was usually used for dead storage. What to my wondering eyes should appear—no, not a shiny red sleigh—but a case of Hennessey Five Star Extra Cognac.

After asking Dad if that was extravagant, I felt pretty good and vindicated.

Standing with Martha and Rene Beland,
Dad is holding two light-color mutations.
Poole Mink Farm went on to specialize exclusively
in natural dark mink and was a member of GLMA,
the Great Lakes Mink Association.

THE MINK FARM

MINK LIFE CYCLE

A mink's life cycle is regulated by length of daylight. March is breeding season, as it is with squirrels, woodchucks, skunks, foxes and other small wild animals. Most young mink are fully grown by late June. By late November mink have shed their summer coats and grown prime winter coats.

BREEDING IN MARCH

When the farm changed from being a hobby to a full time occupation, there were about 200 breeder female mink and 25 breeder males. Breeding season was during the month of March. Pairs were put together, and they would fight a bit in order for the female to ovulate. If they fought too much they would have to be separated.

NEST BOXES

Mink nest boxes were of two different kinds: a larger one for families and breeder males and smaller one for singles growing up. All were made with one-inch wire mesh.

The larger box for mother and kits was divided into two compartments. From the wire cage the mother could enter the first compartment and then go through a hole in the divider into the second compartment where the kits were born and stayed while they were small. As the kits grew, the divider was removed so the litter would still fit in the box.

The smaller kind of box was used for a single young kit to grow in or for a mother mink after kits were taken away.

Standard pens were 36 inches long, 12 inches high and 18 inches wide separated by three inches to prevent fighting. Watering cups fit between the pens.

KITS IN MAY

Kits were born in May. Each morning in order to check new litters in, there were certain signs to look for. Chances were the food was not eaten. Then there might be a black dropping that occurred because the mother mink cleaned up the kits and the afterbirth. Next was to put one's ear up to the nest box, and if all was well hear soft little peeps. Sometimes the kits would be born so fast the mother couldn't keep up with her duties, so two or three kits might become tangled in their umbilical cords. Little newborn kits were half the length of one's little finger and about the same size. Because of this, we would push the mother out of the nest box to check. If there was a tangle we had a pair of fingernail scissors and would delicately snip the kits free.

A second-year mother would usually have more milk than a female kit mother. A kit mother might have three or four babies, but if she had seven or eight or more at least some would go in my pocket and be dropped off with an older female down the line. Once in a while a mother would refuse to take a kit into the nest box, usually because she sensed something wrong with the baby.

Baby mink grew quickly. When only three weeks old their eyes opened and they began to eat real mink food. The nest box filled up rapidly as kits doubled in size. Soon they began to fight and had to be removed from the over-crowded nest box. Mothers were put into an old-female row, kit females into another row, and male kits into a row of their own. In the wild, young kits would start to be on their own.

Each litter had its own record. Date of birth and number of kits were marked on the mother's record card that indicated her age and previous litter history. When bred, the father's number was recorded, so when new breeding stock was selected the ones that produced finer fur got the credit.

From time to time the breeder herd would be improved by new blood lines brought in from other mink farms. Breeding stock was bought and sold as a trio: two females and one male.

SEPARATING IN JUNE

By mid-to-late June seven or eight kits nearly filled the nest box, which was twice the size of a single box. Our crew separated the litter the last week in June.

The crew all wore heavy leather gloves for catching and handling the mink. One brought a nest box out from the darker shed into the sunlight and dumped mother and kits into a 55-gallon steel drum that was cut a bit shorter so we could lean over and reach to its bottom. The mother could jump out, so we had to be ready to catch her and put her into a six-mink carrying crate. When that crate was full, we took it to an old-female row and put each old female in her own pen. Each move included the identifying record.

Then we caught each young one out of the barrel and sexed it—held it up and inspected to determine if it was male or female—then put it into its correct crate: young male or young female. Once in a while when holding a kit, it would wet. This might be while holding the kit up to the light and would be on the worker.

Working the barrel was fun, catching and separating. The entire crew made it efficient: one person brought out litters; another worked the barrel; another, often a young girl, kept records on note cards. For a year or two Martha was the record-keeper, Valerie Johnson was the next one. Other crew members took the crates to the correct empty rows, male or female, and tucked each kit into a new pen. A breeding record card accompanied each young mink to its row and was stapled to its box.

Kits on their own chirped and cried the first few nights, then things settled down.

PELTING IN NOVEMBER

Pelting time, at Thanksgiving, was critical to success.

As the season changed to late fall, little by little a mink became prime, as it grew its winter coat. The last part to grow was the fur that covered the ears. The skin on the inside became creamy white and didn't show black root hairs. A northeast storm could cause a natural dark mink to start turning brown losing its fine near-black color and value.

Skinning
Fleshing
Drying
Packing & Shipping

Neighbor Joe Gallo, fleshing before machines came along

LUNCHES

Because of working hard outdoors in the cold during pelting time, often we would go to Twin Maples for substantial hot lunches. We entered the kitchen through the back door and sat at a table set up just for us. Our mink aromas were confined to the kitchen, leaving the dining room smelling sweet for other regular customers. My mother was relieved that her kitchen stayed sweeter smelling, too.

149

SKINNING

I wasn't at school. I was home for mink pelting. I would be there all day, every day. First we caught mink and put them in a six-compartment crate. The crate was placed in an airtight box containing Cyanogas (cyanide powder) for a few minutes. Dead mink were then put on the pelting table and skinned while still warm: a little knife work cutting open the skin near the back legs, separating the pelt from the body by hand, pulling the pelt inside out, ending with some knife work around the neck and head. It was a dis-assembly line. A smaller female mink could be skinned in about a minute. Larger males took longer and were much harder to skin.

I had (and still have) large hands, so I was good at catching big kit males. I caught each kit around the neck as it ran into its nest box and put it in a crate. If I didn't catch it just right, it chewed on the thumb of my heavy leather mitten. One chew did not reach my thumb, but at the end of the day when the leather was worn through, "OW!"

Skinning crew help was always needed. People came to watch not knowing that the scent would get on their clothes. Mert Tefft was a middle school principal who loved to help when he could. He enjoyed working with men for a change instead of managing mostly women teachers.

For many years the number of mink skinned each day depended on the number of mink that could be fleshed— fleshing being a slower process.

Years later the skinning was done as quickly as possible in order to process the furs at their prime. Then the skinned pelts in bundles of 50 or so were put in large plastic bags and frozen for later fleshing.

FLESHING

In the early years, a pelt was hung upside down and inside out on one of six poles hung from the garage ceiling. A flesher skillfully scraped its fat so as not to expose the root hairs or rip the skin. Then the pelt was placed on a board for drying. A special fleshing crew arrived after supper. Some of the men on the crew worked in the shoe industry in Hudson. It was a chance to earn extra money just before Christmas. Calluses on their hands would slowly disappear thanks to the mink oil.

When freezing became available, instead of having to skin and flesh in the same day, the pelts were frozen and fleshed later in the year when caring for the smaller breeding stock took less time.

Another improvement was the development of a fleshing machine. This had two horizontal poles on a level stand. One person would load pelts, a second person would do the fleshing. No longer did we need a fleshing crew in November. Two people did all the fleshing in December and January.

DRYING

The next step was to put the pelt on a drying board and hang it in the warm cellar. While being put on a drying board the pelt was trimmed so that the buyer could see a patch of fur on the lower back in order to correctly grade it into matching bundles. When drying, the fat came out of the skin and needed to be wiped dry, more than once.

151

PACKING & SHIPPING

At long last the year's crop was ready to go. The last step was to box the dried pelts and send them by Railway Express to Hudson's Bay Company, located in the fur district in New York City. Hudson's Bay Company the oldest company in North America, held monthly auctions to sell trade lots to the furriers, who would then manufacture all sorts of stylish women's wear, such as fur coats, jackets and stoles.

Then I trucked about 15 barrels of carcasses and five barrels of fleshed fat to Woburn, Massachusetts, to a rendering company. The season was over.

Mr. and Mrs. Gentile, our former neighbors, lived close-by the rendering company. On my way home, the Gentiles were always happy when I stopped by for a visit. We chatted of growing up escapades and updates of both families: who was where and what they were doing.

FEEDING MACHINES

Pens were lined up side by side down both sides of each aisle, two aisles in each shed, and altogether measured more than a mile. Up to this time, all feeding had been laboriously done by hand. A new development and vast improvement was the feeding machine.

In order to use a new feeder, on the end of the shed each aisle had to be up-graded so the narrow feeder could both fit and turn around outside. Finally, after the upgrades, we were ready. I wasn't home to see it delivered but was probably off in the truck picking up more fish.

When I got home, there it was: an automated feeder that was a beautiful Caterpillar-yellow—no scratches, no food stains, just a narrow four-wheel cart with a driver's seat high up front and a metal tank on back.

It took three wheelbarrow loads to fill the tank. Food was delivered to the top of each pen through a hand-held two-inch-diameter hose controlled by a micro-switch. The food came out onto the pen sort of like soft serve ice cream, only much faster. The feeder was powered with six heavy-duty six-volt batteries that powered one electric motor for travel and another to run the auger to fill the pump and pump the food out the hose.

On the third day just when we were getting used to it, Dad spoke up, "Order another feeding machine just like it." Once we gave up hand feeding and counted on the machines, we needed back-up in case of a break-down.

The feed room was upgraded with a hoist to help load the feeding machines. Every day after feeding the batteries were plugged in and recharged to be ready for the next day.

In our four double aisled sheds, with two new speedy feeders it was great fun to see which driver could finish first.

Those feeder machines were what enabled our farm to expand until there were almost 950 breeder females, 150 breeder males and, hopefully, about 4,000 kits each year.

Eventually we built an additional compact 340-foot shed designed for 1,000 kit females, mink that grew to be only about half the size of males. This was a single-aisle shed designed with eight-inch wide pens separated by perforated metal dividers, too small for paws to reach through. Water cups were at the end of the pens.

That was the end of expansions to Poole Mink Farm.

One of my hats today,
60 years after graduation...

UNIVERSITY OF VERMONT
fall 1951–spring 1956

FRESHMAN YEAR

My semester at Dean must have done the trick, because I was accepted at the University of Vermont to enter the Civil Engineering program. People think UVM stands for University of Vermont. They are wrong. With all my Latin I skills, I figured out Universitas Verde Montis—the University of the Green Mountains.

I had never visited UVM, so my first view of the college in Burlington was the day I was told to appear. Mom and my friend Larry rode in the car with all my clothes, and I rode my motorcycle.

One of my classmates at Dean, and a close friend, was Jack Van Rye. He had graduated from Dean and gone off to UVM where he flunked out—maybe a little too much beer. Jack was headed back to UVM and would be the only one I knew who would be there.

The first few days of college were a blur, including:

1) Get settled in Buckham Hall, a freshman dorm. Meet other bewildered students.

2) Sign up for classes and pay fees for classes and a dormitory room.

3) Find out where my classes are held and when.

4) Find out details of meal possibilities.

5) Wear freshman beanie so upper classmen could give us a hard time.... All in all, too much to deal with all at once.

6) Eventually settle into a routine.

7) Learn about Burlington, a whole new city that was small and not yet spread out into suburbs. Just outside the city edge was farmland.

Because UVM is a land grant college ROTC (Reserve Officers' Training Course) was a required course. I enrolled in Air Force ROTC and learned how to march, which came in handy later when I was in the Army. I also took a world geography course. There were two kinds of ROTC dress black shoes: regular and officers. They didn't have a regular type that fit me, so I got an officers' pair that polished up better than regular, making it easier to pass inspection.

I enjoyed and was challenged by mechanical drawing three times a week for three hours at a time. English classes were the only ones with a few girls. That's where I met Caroline King. Sometimes she wore a Navy sweatshirt, so I figured it was her boyfriend's and I had no chance. Not so. It belonged to her father, who was Dean of Education, and she had a job at the UVM Dairy Bar. Perfect setup: ICE CREAM SODAS made to order. Caroline was fun, and we dated most of freshman year.

My life as a freshman college student away from home

was a totally new experience.

Dates were usually a movie or some sort of party at the Sigma Alpha Epsilon (SAE) fraternity house, where I was a pledge. Pledges had to work in order to be considered to become a brother. My job for a semester was to call and obtain chaperons, usually a professor, to attend our parties.

The motorcycle wasn't much help in the northland, and by Thanksgiving Larry came to pick up me and the bike. With the front wheel off we rigged a way to attach the bike to a trailer ball hitch. It was much too cold to ride the bike 210 miles—even with shin-guards and a windshield.

Kakewalk was a highlight of the year—it was our Winter Carnival with four days of festivities. The first night was a basketball game, next night was skits put on by four fraternities, the third night was a large formal dance with a major well-known band, and the fourth day was teas put on by sororities and the judging of snow sculptures made by the sororities and fraternities.

Cakewalks originated in the 1850's as entertainment by slaves on Southern plantations and later developed into white and black minstrel shows. At UVM's Kakewalk each fraternity usually entered a two-man team that practiced for days to prepare. Made up in blackface and wearing fancy bright costumes, team members would do a precision dance routine to the strains of "Cotton Babies" that included high kicks together, then separately, then together again. Winners would be awarded a cake. Kakewalk at UVM is no more. Today blackface is considered to be based on racial stereotypes and does not honor the history of African-American slaves in the South.

Outside my freshman dorm was a long parking lot for three dorms. The pride of these dorms was Tanner's "little deuce coupe." When we were supposed to be studying on a warm spring night with the windows open, it was a treat to hear that car open up for a quarter-mile run. Never forgotten!

Another episode involving glass raised its ugly head. In Buckham Hall in the evening when things were quieting down, I took an empty gallon glass jug up to the third floor and used it like a bowling ball, throwing it down the hall. It bounced against the walls, back and forth, making a great noise until it reached the other end and smashed into hundreds of pieces. Meanwhile, I was back in bed in room 213. I don't know why I was a suspect, but Edmund Balducci, the proctor, came into my room and held his hand over my heart to see if my heart was beating at a faster rate or whether I was really asleep as I was pretending to be. Someone had to drive the proctors up the wall.

At home with Martha and Nancy in our Sudbury driveway

SOPHOMORE YEAR & DISASTER

It was much easier to return for my second year, knowing the city, the campus, the routine, and the fraternity house.

However, my sophomore year soon became a DISASTER! I stopped studying. At the end of the first semester I flunked out. I also flunked out of ROTC. I was eligible to be drafted into the Army.

I could get back into college second semester by changing my major, which I did, to Agricultural Economics. As long as I was in college I wouldn't be drafted for Army active duty.

I also joined the National Guard. I joined a medical outfit. One night a week a few of us would go downtown for a Guard meeting. No, I wasn't a doctor. At one of our meetings a different National Guard outfit came to us to receive shots. They were all lined up with a burly sergeant at the front of the line. My lieutenant asked if anyone knew how to give shots. I said I gave them on the mink farm. I thought the sergeant was going to pass out. No problem giving shots.

National Guard: Bill Battles, Joe Newall, me, Curt Burrell

Second semester was an improvement.

Bob Rudd was a fraternity brother. We both had transferred from Civil Engineering to the College of Agriculture. Once in a while I would go for a weekend with Bob to his house in North Pownal, Vermont. It was always a great time there, and I felt right at home.

Bob lived on a dairy farm so we had a lot in common. Our work ethic was similar. I didn't have to get up early to milk the mink, but daily responsibilities to our livestock came first. It was fun to get away from Burlington for a weekend and fill in with the tractor work and haying. We also went deer hunting.

I went out with his sister Betty once in a while. We were not old enough to drink legally in Vermont. But we were close to Hoosick Falls, New York, where the legal drinking age was 18, and we went there for a few beers.

One evening she asked, "Who is going to help with the milking tomorrow morning?"

"I will," said I.

Betty and I got home LATE. I just got to bed and to sleep when I was informed, "It's time to milk."

What fun! I do enjoy my sleep!

Now that Bob and I were no longer in Engineering but had transferred to Agriculture, we were working with animals. Most of the class was quite excited about it. But with Bob's and my background of growing up and working on our farms, we were not. Our assignment was to work with a flock of sheep, pick out the best one and then "fit" it. That meant trim it, clean it, and then show it. Our sheep, Bob's and mine, came in first and second for physical qualities (we knew how to pick them) and last and next to last for fitting and showing.

I knew how to get dates. A dental hygiene course at UVM needed people to work on. I signed up for getting my teeth cleaned. All the dental hygienists were beautiful young women. Clean teeth and no charge was an easy way to get acquainted and thus get a DATE.

Getting back and forth—Vermont and Massachusetts—was difficult. This was before Interstate highways. I tried all kinds of ways: car with relatives, car with other students, airplane to Boston, overnight bus, hitchhiking, motorcycle and my own car. It was more than five-and-a-half hours by car. Without riding any faster, the motorcycle would take a just little more than four hours. You didn't have to slow down for corners and could get through traffic and pass cars much easier and faster, though you were at the mercy of the weather. When it was cold, newspaper rolled up around your legs under your pants helped a lot. I tried to get World War II electric heated gloves that were used by bomber pilots. Failed!

At the end of the second semester I put in for a transfer from National Guard because I was going home for the summer to work on the farm. The transfer finally came through in late August, but by then it was almost time to return to Burlington, so the transfer was canceled.

Between sophomore and junior year I met Eddie Brown. His father had an auto body shop so it was easy for Eddie to change cars—more than 30 different ones that year. I liked his 1939 Mercury Convertible. He liked my '39 Harley 74. We traded . 1939 was the first year that Mercuries came on the market. They were really overgrown Fords. Larry helped me get it back in shape: dual exhaust, high-compression heads, motor bored out and Lincoln Zephyr gears. Ninety miles per hour in second gear, it had a flat-head V-8 engine that really purred.

161

THE TIME HAS COME TO BACK UP
AND FILL IN THE GAPS

Mom took care of Grampa Poole. He came to live with us in Sudbury after Gramma died and soon after Nancy and I had traveled to visit him in Iowa. After Grampa died in September 1951, when I began my sophomore year in college, is the lowest point in this saga.

Dad left to travel to Reno, Nevada, to obtain a DIVORCE. We were devastated. The hardest part for me was to see Mom so hurt. Dad and I had worked together since before I went to first grade. My relationship with him became strained. I didn't care how I approached daily life.

Meanwhile, back to Burlington, by the end of first semester it became time to stop feeling sorry for myself. It was, and still is, the absolute lowest part of my life. Some things, such as death, are very sad but part of life. When actions are sinful and hurtful they are difficult to excuse. I try to understand forgiveness. Maybe some day I will. When Dad died in 1962 there were two funeral ceremonies—two different families, but never the two should meet.

That time was much worse than later when my wife, Wendy, died. She had been an active member of Water of Life Lutheran Church in Newcastle, Maine. That was a sad time, but it didn't seem as though it was against God's will.

JUNIOR YEAR

September was approaching, another semester at college.

For the first time I had a car, so travel arrangements were much easier. Living in the fraternity house, 56 Summit Street, Burlington, Vermont, was where I was. We had our own cook, so eating meals there was much better than at the college cafeteria or local restaurants.

Bob Rudd bought a motorcycle. There are Harley fans and English or other foreign bike fans, but never the two should meet. He bought a an English Triumph TR110. We drove to North Pownal to pick it up. Robert, his father, wanted me to ride it back. I said no, because it had a hand clutch and foot shift, opposite controls from my Harley. He prevailed. I rode.

We were still in North Pownal, and I was coming to a 90-degree left turn and couldn't slow down. Instead of turning, I went straight up a driveway. So far so good. The next hurdle was a parked car. Look, there is enough room between the car and the back step. I squeezed through. The following hurdle? A chicken yard! Insurmountable! I laid the bike down and slid into the chicken-yard fence.

Hens: Safe

Motorcycle: One bent handle bar

Me: Feelings hurt

163

BLIND DATE WITH WENDY
(ANNA WENDEL WAHLERS)

Joe, an SAE brother, was dating Sally Shepardson, a young woman at Skidmore College in Saratoga Springs, New York. Skidmore Junior Weekend was coming up, and Sally needed a date for her roommate. Would I travel 120 miles to Skidmore for a whole weekend for a blind date?

Scary! What if we didn't get along? The deal was done!

I met Wendy Wahlers. It wasn't love at first sight, but we did have a GREAT TIME. Back at 56 Summit Street, my roommates were surprised that a blind date had turned out so well!

Why was someone like Wendy not already going steady? There had to be other weekend dates. Letters soon were traveling between Saratoga Springs and Burlington. My life was on the rise. The only problem was how to see each other on the weekends. I began studying in a different manner, as though it really mattered, which it did!

Young people used to meet others within a five-mile radius—next came extending to other towns. I was a young man from Massachusetts in school in Vermont getting acquainted with a young woman from New Jersey attending Skidmore College in Saratoga Springs, New York. Things looked much greener 120 miles away.

Phone calls were only for special occasions. *No iPads or computers, yet we survived.* It was a challenge to meet someone in a strange place when a suitable place for meeting was not known.

Again, I was really blessed.

SONG FROM THE SKIDMORE COLLEGE JUNIOR CLASS ANNUAL SHOW

Robots do all our work each day
We get milk from the milky-way
Modern life is great in 3000 A.D.

Atomic rocket ships
For our celestial trips
Why don't you join us and see?

Music with supersonic tone
Brings the men here from every zone
For a co-ed interspacial spree

Five–D is here to stay
We go to Mars to play
Just think how happy you'll be

Paris once used to be the fad
When our men were so bold and bad
Venus now holds charm for moderns like we

We govern every star
Whether it be near or far
All systems planetary

Here's a glimpse at a future age
As we now show it on the stage
Life is really great in 3000 A.D.

PANTY RAID

It was spring, and the big college rage was panty raids.

Ours started out slowly, but as more police showed up the students felt that they should give them what they were looking for. One guy called a cop a woodchuck, and he promptly got a billy club knock on his head and was hauled away in a cruiser. The National Guard was called out as well as the local police and fire departments. Water hoses moved back crowds, and tear gas was used on the green. I shut my eyes and ran away from the tear gas full speed ahead. Didn't matter that I might run into a tree. Some girls threw panties out their windows.

Then it was over as fast as it had started.

CUT HAND

One of the bathrooms in the fraternity house had a damaged window. After a shower the mirror was steamed up and I wanted to use it to shave. The window was stuck, and when I tried to raise it the glass came apart and I ended up with a nasty cut on the palm of my right hand. As it healed it resulted in a patch of dead skin with a BAD dead-skin smell.

That was just when I would be meeting Wendy's parents for the first time. What a nice first impression!

ENGAGEMENT RING

Soon Wendy and I were engaged to be married.

I bought a ring and had plans of when to give it to her. We were traveling to Maplewood, New Jersey, to visit her parents. That would be the time.

The problem was that the ring burned a hole in my pocket. I didn't wait until we reached 109 Oakview Avenue.

WENDY'S SKIDMORE GRADUATION

The next highlights were our graduations, which were one day apart in May of 1956.

Skidmore's was first. I attended, sat proudly with Wendy's parents and the rest of her family at the ceremony and stayed for some of the extended festivities.

MY UVM GRADUATION

Late that day I traveled back to Burlington for my own graduation from the University of Vermont the next day.

Mom, Nancy and Martha had driven up from Sudbury and were there to see me in cap and gown.

Diploma in hand at ceremony's end, I headed for home with my Mercury packed with belongings. Martha, who had a bad case of poison ivy, rode with me. Nancy and Mom followed in Mom's car and did their best to keep up.

NEWLYWEDS IN SUNNY ISLES: Mr. and Mrs. James Poole of Landham road, South Sudbury, Mass., are pictured here outside "Mizzentop", the guest house in Warwick, Bermuda, where they spent their honeymoon. Mrs. Poole is the former Wendy Wahlers, daughter of Mr. and Mrs. D. F. Wahlers of Maplewood, New Jersey. Mr. Poole is a mink rancher in South Sudbury.

170

WEDDING

After graduation, it was back to the mink farm for me.

Wendy had a job at Georg Jensen in New York City designing product displays and windows. I was in Sudbury.

Our wedding plans included a ceremony and reception on September 29, 1956. Finally the day arrived.

We were married in the Lutheran Church in Maplewood. After a honeymoon in Bermuda, we moved briefly into the house at the mink farm. Wendy, the artist, made the house a colorful and welcoming home.

UNITED STATES ARMY
1956–1958

HARDSHIP CASE
& ARMY INDUCTION

Guess what! Uncle Sam still wanted me.

In 1956 most draftees entered the Army in September or sooner. Dad contacted the Red Cross because I was needed for pelting season. They listened to him and agreed.

As a hardship case I was inducted into the Army at the Boston Army Base, but not until December.

Induction day was a long: physical exam lines, lines, lines, lines and then—talk about a slow boat to China—a train ride from Boston to Fort Dix, New Jersey. We arrived at Fort Dix at 3 a.m. with sergeants telling us to go back and forth to different places. I lay down under a bush to sleep. At 9 a.m. I was assigned a bunk.

BASIC TRAINING, FORT DIX

My Army career started as basic training at Fort Dix in New Jersey. This was the first time that I felt different than most of the other men in my barracks. There I was: a college graduate and married. A sergeant barking orders did not have much effect on me. Most of the other draftees were young, just out of high school, away from home for the first time and newly subject to orders. I became a father figure, not so fazed by all the rules and regulations.

Meanwhile, back at the farm, Wendy had left Sudbury and returned to Maplewood to get a job and live with her parents, Dietrich and Anna Wahlers.

I was under the care of Sgt. Gillis. If I were ever in combat he would be the one I would pick to serve under. The other platoons felt sorry for us. Sgt. Gillis was scary looking, but he looked out for us. I often wonder about him.

One night we were bussed 10 miles out to a range for training. We had to crawl through a course under barbwire with live machine gun fire over us. They fired over a shallow valley. Every fourth or fifth round was an incendiary round. I was halfway through the course and got these terrific stomach pains, so bad that I thought if I could just stand up that would solve the problem. I wasn't worried about the gunfire, but the stomach pain was awful. I finished the course and immediately headed for the woods. Now I wondered if everyone else would finish the course, get on the bus and leave me out in the middle of nowhere for the rest of the night without my pup tent.

As it was, everything turned out O.K. I enjoyed my bus ride back to the barracks. At the end of basic training we were offered a choice of advanced training. Choices were not guaranteed.

I chose airplane mechanic, and I got my choice. During my Fort Dix tour of basic training I did get to see Wendy briefly, on a Sunday afternoon.

Now I was headed with Ed *(try as I might, I cannot remember Ed's last name)* to Fort Rucker, Alabama, for a course in airplane mechanics. The class was six or eight weeks long. Ed was a Rhodes scholar, probably the only other college graduate, and I think they didn't know where to assign him so he went with me. After this initial assignment I was selected for an advanced course. I chose fixed wing—Ed was still with me. I was getting marks of high 90's without much studying, but Ed was struggling. He was then assigned to the library.

BOARD SIX:
FIXED WING & ROTARY WING

Wendy was still working in New York City, and it hadn't made much sense to have her join me until I had a permanent assignment. At the end of school I was assigned to Board Six, the center of Army Aviation on the other side of Fort Rucker, and not sent to some more exotic place.

As an airplane mechanic it was possible to be assigned to maintain a plane at a U.S. Embassy. Most embassies were assigned a small business twin. A mechanic at an embassy post would be expected to attend all the evening parties and functions in a class one uniform.

Don't worry, Board Six was not like that. We were a small test outfit with both fixed wing and rotary wing machines. We had a Beaver, an Otter, a high wing Aero Commander and two Beechcraft plus an amphibious Cessna Bird Dog Cessna with Edo floats. Some of these were tested to assess their short field take-off and landing capabilities.

As a member of Board Six, I was in the Continental Army on detached duty to Fort Rucker, Alabama. The rest of Board Six was in Washington, D.C. I enjoyed being a crew chief but didn't want to have an Army career.

TEST FLIGHTS

Crew chiefs were responsible for performing serious periodic inspections and, after signing off in the plane's logbook, were required to accompany the pilot on the test flight.

One day Southern Airways was working on the landing gear of an L19 Cessna Bird Dog. I was crew chief. Whenever work was done on landing gear a retraction test had to be performed before signing off in the logbook. Southern Airways did not perform the retraction test. The plane took off from land, and one side wheel went up and the other side stayed down. BAD. The ground crew finally foamed an area off the runway. The pilot put the landing gear in a neutral position and came in very slowly, just barely hanging on the prop. It was a GOOD landing.

The next tests were set up to determine how short a runway they could land in. The problem with the test was that at touchdown the pilot would slam on the brakes, often locking up and blowing a tire. I would have to go out close to the active runway and change the blown-out tire.

SPEC III IN CHARGE

One night I had charge of Quarters (CQ) at the airfield. Many pilots flew in the evening to receive flight hours in order to qualify for flight pay. A plane was taxiing in, so I went out with the flashlights to guide it in. This was so it wouldn't collide with other parked planes and would end up in position to be tied down.

When giving instructions, one is responsible. The lieutenant pilot was not following my instructions. So I waved him off, and I walked away. When he came in on his own I was angry and chewed him out. Definitely a no-no—a spec III does NOT chew out a lieutenant.

After he left I had to move the plane so it could be tied down on the permanent tie-downs. The next morning I expected to be called in for my actions, but it turned out that the whole incident was over.

WENDY JOINED ME &
WE GOT SCHNITZEL

Finally I was settled in one place so Wendy was able to join me. We rented a nice small cottage in Dothan, Alabama, and bought a cute little red dachshund puppy, Schnitzel. His mother was Lovable Lakeside Lady. How could we go wrong?

As Schnitzel grew up that summer it was hot. We lived on a quiet road. He would disappear from time to time. We finally discovered that he would sneak through the shrubs, go down a couple houses and then cross the road. A nice old couple invited him in to nap on a chaise lounge in their AIR CONDITIONED porch.

I BECAME A LUTHERAN

I went to classes and became a Lutheran. Wendy was pleased. The local Lutheran Church had a retired pastor, Henry Meyer. I had been Christened as a baby, but the Lutherans (and Wendy) wanted me Baptized. Trinity Lutheran Church was small, but we had a large confirmation class. I recognized one of my classmates: Perry Gary was a civilian instructor in one of my engine courses.

MORE SNAKES

One night Wendy and I went for a drive to Court Square in Dothan. There were many people buzzing around. What was going on? We parked and went to see. It was springtime when all sorts of creatures come to life after winter naps and was quite a sight!

RATTLESNAKES! Dead ones lined up on the sidewalk all in a row by size, long ones down to short ones. Some live ones were in cages at chest level. When the cage was jiggled, live snakes would buzz. As people peered into the cages a little boy touched their ankles with a stick. World record jumps! What a great reaction.

COMMUTE

Daleville and Fort Rucker were about 20 miles from Dothan. Two or three of us shared rides back and forth to the airfield. As mentioned, Fort Rucker was the center of Army Aviation.

The Fort itself consisted of all the things an Army Post should have. Board Six had the helicopter section there.

Fixed wing was five or six miles away at the airport. The school for Army student pilots was at the airport. All day long Cessna Bird Dogs would be practicing touch-and-goes. We mechanics would talk them down, but they would not listen. The helicopters would play follow the leader. They were much closer. I've forgotten the model number they flew, but it was just like the ones in MASH. They would take off and hover in place, then eight or so would line up in a row. Those pilots became Warrant Officers.

A VISION

Dothan has a circular highway around its perimeter. We lived about half a mile from the highway. I once awoke from a sound sleep around 1 a.m. It wasn't a sound that woke me, but it was the feeling of a presence. Wendy was with me but did not wake up. This presence was wearing a colorful robe and assured me that everything was all right and not to worry. It wasn't a dream. I was wide awake. I thought it might be Jesus. This presence then disappeared and I woke Wendy. In a few minutes we heard sirens and vehicles drive by toward the highway. The next morning we determined that there had been a fatal accident on the highway.

I'm sure we have all been in a situation where we didn't act until much too late. With me it was that I should have contacted the family of the person who died to tell them that things were O.K. I still wonder.

HARDSHIP CASE, AGAIN

Our stay in Dothan was nearing an end. Wendy was pregnant and the baby was due in late October. It looked like we would have a southern cracker, since I was due to be discharged in December.

Again I became a hardship case. Dad and the Red Cross wanted me home three months early in time for pelting season and in time for our baby to be born in Sudbury, Massachusetts, instead of Dothan, Alabama.

Dad prevailed once more. We were going home.

DOTHAN TO SUDBURY

It was time to head for home. It was much more than just a ride in a 1951 blue Ford sedan pulling a U-Haul trailer. It was a major change in Wendy's and my lives. Some men who were drafted when I was were required to serve in the active reserve. My date of entry into the service was when I joined the National Guard. When I was discharged in early October 1958, it was under a different law. I didn't have to serve any Army Reserve time.

We stopped in Washington, D.C., to visit a friend. Schnitzel was left in the hotel room while we went out to dinner. He shredded a large pine cone to keep busy. When we returned, it was a mess all over the room.

Our next stop was 109 Oakview Avenue in Maplewood, New Jersey, to visit Wendy's parents.

The end of our 21-month episode followed. Our mink farm home was waiting for us, with barely enough time to get settled before Dirk Daniel Poole arrived on October 22, 1958. He wouldn't settle down on his first night home. Wendy was nervous.

I said, "Let me hold him," and he settled right down. He needed to be held tighter. He wouldn't break.

Schnitzel arrived at the mink farm upset with the whole world. He did not agree with travel and strange places. But he soon settled into being a mink dog. If a mink was loose in the yard he would drive it out from under pens so we could catch it. He once barked so we knew a mink was loose and hiding in a large pile of nest boxes. He drove it out but didn't see that I then caught it and put it back in its correct box. Later Schnitzel barked at the correct box—one of 4,000—to let us know that he knew all was well.

Schnitzel also took on the responsibility for guarding Dirk when Dirk was napping in the sun on the porch.

181

Me, Dirk and Wendy

HOME

HOME AGAIN & BLESSED

Wendy and I had been on quite a merry-go-round. We had started to learn what life together was all about. College was over for both of us—time for another phase. We had a brand new little boy, Dirk Daniel, to love and take care of.

What would be next? We became members of the Lutheran Church of Framingham with many new friends to meet and to love as a new family.

It's late afternoon and I'm sitting here in Maine again on a dark November Saturday, close to the woodstove. It's windy and cold outside. My long story—memories of growing up, moving away and returning to Sudbury—is done.

I certainly am... blessed.

—Jim Poole

Made in the USA
Middletown, DE
12 January 2017